Carol Shields's
The Stone Diaries

CONTINUUM CONTEMPORARIES

Also available in this series

Barbara Kingsolver's *The Poisonwood Bible*, by Linda Wagner-Martin
Pat Barker's *Regeneration*, by Karin Westman
Kazuo Ishiguro's *The Remains of the Day*, by Adam Parkes
J. K. Rowling's *Harry Potter Novels*, by Philip Nel
Jane Smiley's *A Thousand Acres*, by Susan Farrell
Louis De Bernieres's *Captain Corelli's Mandolin*, by Con Coroneos
Irvine Welsh's *Trainspotting*, by Robert Morace
Toni Morrison's *Paradise*, by Kelly Reames
Donna Tartt's *The Secret History*, by Tracy Hargreaves

Forthcoming in this series

Annie Proulx's *The Shipping News*, by Aliki Varvogli
Kate Atkinson's *Behind the Scenes at the Museum*, by Emma Parker
Haruki Murakami's *The Wind-up Bird Chronicle*, by Matthew Strecher
Jonathan Coe's *What a Carve Up!*, by Pamela Thurschwell
Don DeLillo's *Underworld*, by John Duvall
Graham Swift's *Last Orders*, by Pamela Cooper
Michael Ondaatje's *The English Patient*, by John Bolland
Ian Rankin's *Black and Blue*, by Gill Plain
Brett Easton Ellis's *American Psycho*, by Julian Murphet
Cormac McCarthy's *All the Pretty Horses*, by Stephen Tatum
Iain Banks's *Complicity*, by Cairns Craig
A. S. Byatt's *Possession*, by Catherine Burgass
David Guterson's *Snow Falling on Cedars*, by Jennifer Haytock
Helen Fielding's *Bridget Jones's Diary*, by Imelda Whelehan
Sebastian Faulks's *Birdsong*, by Pat Wheeler
Hanif Kureishi's *The Buddha of Suburbia*, by Nahem Yousaf
Nick Hornby's *High Fidelity*, by Joanne Knowles
Zadie Smith's *White Teeth*, by Claire Squires
Arundhati Roy's *The God of Small Things*, by Julie Mullaney
Alan Warner's *Morvern Callar*, by Sophy Dale
Vikram Seth's *A Suitable Boy*, by Angela Atkins
Margaret Atwood's *Alias Grace*, by Gina Wisker

· CAROL SHIELDS'S

The
Stone
Diaries

A READER'S GUIDE

ABBY WERLOCK

CONTINUUM | NEW YORK | LONDON

2001

The Continuum International Publishing Group Inc
370 Lexington Avenue, New York, NY 10017

The Continuum International Publishing Group Ltd
The Tower Building, 11 York Road, London SE1 7NX

Printed in the United States of America

Library of Congress Cataloging-in-Publication Data

ISBN 0-8264-5249-3

Contents

1.

The Novelist   7

2.

The Novel   18

3.

The Novel's Reception   69

4.

The Novel's Performance   76

5.

Further Reading and Discussion Questions   80

Notes   88

Bibliography   91

The Novelist

Carol Shields holds dual citizenship in both Canada and the United States, and her novel *The Stone Diaries* won awards in both countries—the prestigious Canadian Governor General's Award and the American Pulitzer Prize. She was born Carol Ann Warner on June 2, 1935, to Inez and Robert Warner, in Oak Park, Illinois. Living with her parents, a teacher and a businessman, she grew up in Oak Park until she matriculated at Hanover College in 1953. Oak Park was home to a number of illustrious Americans, including James T. Farrell, author of the Studs Lonigan trilogy; Edgar Rice Burroughs, author of the Tarzan series; Frank Lloyd Wright, the influential architect; and Ernest Hemingway, who set the course for much of literature in the twentieth century. At one point Shields's parents boarded with Hemingway's parents, and, later, as a writer, she says she could never understand her parents' lack of interest in reading the famous Modernist writer.[1]

With her marriage to Donald Shields, a Canadian engineering student whom she met while both were studying in England at Exeter University, Carol Shields left the United States to live in Canada. Having lived there since she was twenty-two, Shields considers herself Canadian. Because she was reared and educated in the United States, however, she likes to think of herself as having one foot firmly planted on either side of the border. As her husband completed his doctorate and became a professor of engineering, much of her married life involved a number of moves throughout Canada—Toronto, Ottawa, Winnipeg, and, most recently Victoria—as well as sabbaticals and travels abroad, particularly to England and France. They have five children—four girls and a boy—and Shields's literary achievements are all the more impressive for the way she has broken the stereotype: She has been married to the same man for forty-three years, she has managed to publish some twenty volumes in every major literary genre, and she has taught at the university level. In addition to her work as a professor of English and creative writing, Shields served four years as chancellor at the University of Manitoba before moving to Victoria in 1999. She believes in happiness and in supportive family relationships. In an interview with Donna Hollenberg, Shields observes, "I remember being spooked by Tillie Olsen's essay on women writers in which she said that we have had no great women writers who have been mothers or who have been part of an involving marriage. . . . I'm not sure I agree. . . . A secure, loving family has sustained me and given me perspective, even though I know how family life consumes and fractures time" (Hollenberg 3). Shields then, has managed to achieve her successes despite marrying right after her college graduation and raising a large family. As a result, her fiction tends to be more optimistic than that of some of her compatriots.

Shields has commented often on the encouragement she received from her own parents while growing up. She read voraciously as a child, and has cited the books that she loved: the Bobbsey Twins, *Anne of Green Gables, The Five Little Peppers, Tales of the Limberlost,* and other childhood favorites of American children in the 1940s and 1950s. She lists among her influences

Gabriella Roy (who grew up in Manitoba), Jane Austen, Alice Munro, Mavis Gallant, Virginia Woolf, and Philip Larkin. Although she now views her midwestern childhood as insular, it provided her with a certain security that seems to shine from the pages of her fiction. She graduated from Hanover College in 1957, with a major in English and a minor in history. She qualified for a teaching license "so I would have something to fall back on, if I were widowed or divorced, or failed to find a husband."[2] These reminiscences of "the way it was" growing up in the 1950s, color *The Stone Diaries* in an initially nostalgic way, but ultimately this nostalgia becomes ironic and even despairing, mitigated but not alleviated by the heroine's optimism and ability to survive.

"My mother played golf before she married," recalls Shields, "in fact, my father courted her on the golf course—but as a child I had trouble picturing her doing anything but being a mother—she had stopped playing golf after her marriage because there simply wasn't time. I think," she says musingly, "that so many people passed their whole lives without having a real conversation. And of course I never talked with my father . . . in those days there were so many taboos, and so many things were emotionally freighted." And then, in a changed tone, she remarks, "How different we are today—young people talk about anything! Just recently my father-in-law, who's a dear man, looked a bit shocked when the conversation turned to vasectomies, but I could tell he was thrilled that we can talk about these things now."[3] Shields has learned from her mother-in-law, too, incorporating one of her stories into *The Stone Diaries*: "My mother-in-law told me about the old Jewish peddler. She was hesitant, because we're all so aware of political correctness these days, but she recalls that after he would leave the farmhouse, people really would boil the cup because of the fear of germs. Helpful to me in writing this difficult scene was seeing a San Francisco play called *Rediscovering Aunt Jemimah*, a play that deconstructs the old stereotypes. I tried, though, to include both historical and family context, so I hope that no one is offended."

Shields took a magazine writing course at the University of Toronto and sold stories to both the Canadian Broadcasting Company (CBC) and the British Broadcasting Company (BBC), and in her late twenties returned to writing poetry, winning her first award, for poetry, in 1965. She then wrote a thesis on the nineteenth-century Canadian writer Susannah Moodie, earning her M. A. in English at the University of Ottawa while she published her first two novels, *Small Ceremonies* and *The Box Garden*. Today, Shields is considered one of Canada's foremost authors.

Her first novel, *Small Ceremonies* (1976), follows the lives of Judith and Martin Gill, a husband and wife who, despite their mutual affection, actually know very little about each other. Judith Gill, like Shields, is writing the biography of Susannah Moodie, and her husband Jack is a historian. *The Box Garden* (1977) takes up the story of Charleen, Judith Gill's sister. *Happenstance* (1980), and A *Fairly Conventional Woman* (1982), eventually issued in one volume, portray the different perspectives of Brenda, a quilt maker and her husband Jack Bowman, a historian, during a single weekend. Of all her characters, Shields says that she most identifies with those like Jack, "the observer," or with the protagonist of *Small Ceremonies*, who says, "I am a watcher. My own life will never be enough for me." And indeed, as a closely watchful observer Shields has given us the realistic portraits of such characters as Daisy Goodwill Flett in *The Stone Diaries* (Gussow 2).

These novels were followed by *Various Miracles* (1985), a collection of short stories in which Shields experimented with form, and *Swann* (1987), a literary whodunit generally credited as a turning point in her fiction. Shields remarks, "Although I think I was changing my style and approach with *Happenstance*, it's basically true that the big change occurred with *Swann*. I never got it quite the way I wanted, but I knew I had a different kind of book. This encountered some resistance from the publisher, but I knew what I wanted. It's definitely my favorite book—I felt full of confidence that the novel could be bent in any direction, read from multiple perspectives. I had been reading quite a bit of postmodern criticism at that time. No, I don't read much of it today—in fact, I was at a dinner party just last night where we discussed the question, 'Is it over?' Everyone has different views, of course."

The Orange Fish (1990) contained more short stories in the post-modern fashion, illuminated by Shields's hallmark slanted perspective, and was followed by *Departures and Arrivals* (1990), a play. Although Shields is clearly best known for her novels, she thoroughly enjoys writing the plays, which she says always get her "off the ground" because they "have more of a surreal edge to them." Whereas a writer must pay close attention to consistency of tone in a novel, she feels she "can do anything on stage." Shields adds, "I like theatre that is theatrical. I love people tap-dancing across the stage."[4]

Returning to the novel, Shields collaborated with Blanche Howard on *A Celibate Season* (1991), an epistolary novel, followed by *The Republic of Love* (1992), in which two very unlikely late twentieth-century protagonists fall deeply and romantically in love with each other.

She returned to poetry with *Coming to Canada* (1992) and to drama with *Thirteen Hands* (1993), a play about three generations of bridge players that opened at Toronto's Alumni Theater, then published *The Stone Diaries*. *Larry's Party* (1997), a novel published to much acclaim, closely looks at life from a late twentieth-century male perspective. It was followed by the story collection *Dressing Up for the Carnival* (2000), full of insights into the way we wear costumes as we enter different parts of our lives. The next year saw the publication of a biography, *Jane Austen* (2001), and a collection of essays, *Dropped Threads* (2001) that Shields co-edited with Marjorie

Anderson. This essay collection has enjoyed notable success, remaining for weeks on the nonfiction bestselling list in Canada. Shields is currently working on a novel that she has entitled *Unless*.

Critics have consistently praised Shields' work, particularly her "superb descriptive powers and ability to capture the nature of everyday life," comparing her with such writers as A. S. Byatt, Margaret Atwood, and Alice Munro."[5] Some question her feminism, but Shields, whose work displays an unquestionable interest in women, is equally interested in men, in the human complexity that applies to both sexes, and states unequivocally that "men are just as complicated as women." Rather than poke fun at men or academics, Shields says, "I'm told that my writing often reflects academic pursuits, but I haven't (yet) written a genuine academic novel, and probably won't."[6] She goes on to say she'd like to write one that praised rather than satirized the academy (Hollenberg 4, 5).

This sentiment is characteristic of Carol Shields: she has a kindly, sympathetic view of human nature that, like her feminism, risks being unfashionable because she refuses to insult her readers or impugn her male characters. She is modest, too, and frank about her output, revealing that on a good day she might write up to three pages, and in her afterword to the recently published *Dropped Threads*, describes the luxury of spending an entire October afternoon reworking one sentence (345). Never the prima donna, Shields loves collaborating, and, in addition to work with David Williamson on the play *Anniversary* (1998) and with Blanche Howard on the epistolary novel *A Celibate Season*, she has collaborated on a short story with her daughter Anne and a play with her daughter Catherine.

Shields works in numerous genres and has published several volumes of poetry justifiably praised for the poignant, reflective, wistful voice exemplified in *Coming to Canada* and the earlier volumes, *Others* (1972) and *Intersect* (1974). She feels most comfortable with novels, however,[7] perhaps because she needs the time and space to draw out her characters who, like Anne Tyler's, are those who might otherwise be overlooked (Gussow 2). She takes seriously the structures and ceremonies that help give cohesion to her characters' lives, and she honestly believes that "people can and do re-invent themselves, so that's part of the life story" (Sturino 177). "I'm also interested in the randomness of the world and the synchronicities that occur," she tells Joanne Kaufman, and the degree to which we can tell our life stories with truthfulness: "You've always got an unreliable narrator, so much gets enhanced, so much gets erased, so much has to be imagined" (Kaufman 32).

As is obvious with any of her books, particularly *The Stone Diaries*, "the use of imagination is terribly important. That's why we read novels, learn about other lives, to enhance our own—otherwise, we'd just be getting a peek at life through this slit. I like to step out of my own consciousness and into someone else's; I do it so often, it's as if they see me coming—'Oh, not her again!' Everyone does this—it's hard work, you never get a day off."

Overall Shields's work is identified with postmodernist themes: mother-daughter symbiosis, husband-wife estrangement; the inventiveness and role of the writer; the occasional silliness of the professoriate; loneliness and our resulting frustration; the tension between free will and chance: and, perhaps most memorably for her readers, those rare moments when we transcend all this and recognize and value our common humanity.[8] Her themes are not just love, courtship, and marriage, but also children and the nature of male and female sensuality, compared and contrasted (Gillespie 62). And again, Shields believes in the possibility of happiness. At times she displays a wry wit, too, sometimes characterized as "a form of black humor that incites a giggle just because it so categorically refuses to romanticize the situation. Absurdity, satire, paradox, and mistaken identity are also the source of much pleasure" (Solomon 1).

Recalling her first publication in the United States, Shields displays her characteristic wit: "I recall never having heard of *Kirkus Reviews* and assuming it had to do with Kirkus, in upstate New York. 'How nice,' I thought, after publishing *Small Ceremonies*, "that this little town is reviewing my book!" She enjoyed writing some of the humorous exchanges and perspectives in *The Stone Diaries*: "It was fun to write those various versions of other people's impressions through Daisy's eyes, and the lists of advice, as in the advice before the Orkney Island trip. I guess I feel that life is rich in comedy."

Shields has written an illuminating article on the technique of structure and the integral way she uses it in her fiction. She believes that "certain traditional structures have lost their relevance"[9] and she bases her own structures on the way women talk among each other, seeming to digress but actually telling side stories integral to the main story. This experimentation with technique helped her to find "new and possibly subversive structures" ("Framing the Structure," 3). More and more she used domestic detail which, as part of our daily lives, deserves to be placed in the novel rather than shoved aside as it has been by too many fiction writers. And she completely "abandoned Chekov's dictum that if there is a rifle hanging over the fireplace, it must go off before the story ends" ("Structure," 3). In this way she has gradually used structure as the "narrative bones" that can at least partially replace plot, a contrivance that she increasingly distrusts ("Structure," 3).

She has a clear vision of the ways she put together each of her novels. *Small Circumstances* was framed by the academic year, September through May, and Shields used images of boxcars to keep herself "sane" as she filled them up and sent them through the timeline ("Structure," 2). For *The Box Garden* she used the seven days of the week, envisioning them as seven wire coat hangers from which she would suspend material. For *Swann* she used the idea of four independent novellas that she concluded with a playlike dramatization. Similarly, *The Republic of Love* is comprised of one-week segments stretching from Easter to Christmas, alternating between the two lovers, Fay and Tom. *The Stone Diaries* is based on the image of a small series of Chinese nesting boxes.

When asked whether she intended the name of *The Stone Diaries* protagonist as a subversion of earlier fictional heroines named Daisy, Shields responds that if there are influences "from Henry James (Daisy Miller) or Scott Fitzgerald (Daisy Buchanan), it's at a subconscious level. I have always had trouble with names—I like to keep them short, so when I came up with Daisy, I liked it—it's a flower name, and it's short and easy to use. And I had used it before, in *Swann*." The entire subject of influences seems to intrigue her. She continues, "I have a 'bibliotherapist' friend who gave me Harriet Doerr's *Stones for Ibarra* to read . . . no, I didn't feel that she consciously influenced me, but I think these things are in the drinking water, don't you?" When asked about her use of flowers and gardens, Shields responds in an amused voice: "Yes, gardens appear often in my books. I'm interested in the way in which the natural world is divided and subdivided. I had four aunts who each had very different gardens—but I'm not much of a gardener myself. It's strange, because I'm frequently asked to write about gardens, and I actually did write one article on gardens."

Shortly after winning the Pulitzer Prize for *The Stone Diaries*, she instituted the Carol Shields Winnipeg Book Award, a $2,000 annual prize open to any work of fiction, nonfiction, poetry, or drama that contributes to the appreciation of life in the city (*Maclean's* 1). Her winning the Pulitzer Prize, as several critics point out, puts Shields in the company of such past winners as John Cheever, William Faulkner, Ernest Hemingway, John Updike, and Edith Wharton, to name only a few. When asked whether, like Edith Wharton—or even Hemingway—she relies on readers to help fill in the gaps in the narrative, Shields replies, "When I was planning *The Stone*

Diaries, I intentionally wrote in the gaps. My idea was to cut into the life of Daisy every 10 years or so; I knew that meant I would miss certain important moments such as childbirth, education, sexual initiation, but I could catch other things that were going on." Although Shields says she was "randomly" selecting certain phases of Daisy's life, she believes that "a lot of women do have these gaps in their lives that have to be filled in. Students are always shocked when, on the first day of class, I ask them to write a creative autobiography: 'What?!' they say, thinking that a life story must be chronological and factual."

Biography, of course, is Shields's "obsession," and it constitutes a major issue in *The Stone Diaries*. "Daisy," says Shields, "continues to revise herself . . . and that's an issue that autobiography raises: how much can we alter, revise, subtract? She's made up of all these people's impressions, so her real identity is a big question mark in her head." *The Stone Diaries*, she says, is "the saddest book I've ever written. But at that time I was healthy, and grateful that I had a creative, productive middle age—something many women in my generation, as well as my mother's, didn't have." Regarding the men overshadowing Daisy, she remarks, "I do think women were overshadowed then, of course, and I think they are overshadowed today. I don't think women have much of a chance, and my daughter Anne Giardino has just written an article on this subject in *Dropped Threads*," the essay collection that Shields co-edited with Marjorie Anderson.

In the fall of 1998, Shields was diagnosed with breast cancer and underwent a mastectomy and chemotherapy. "I suppose we all have something to reach for during times of emotional bankruptcy, times of loss. I've come to a certain sense of peace with this disease, about where it's going to lead."[10] The summer of 1999 marked her last year as chancellor at the University of Manitoba; Shields says that she grew accustomed to "being a woman with cancer," but, after twenty years in Winnipeg, she admits that "the winters get harder as you get older," and she and her husband Don decided to move to Victoria where, Don adds, Carol will have a house, something she's "always wanted" to return to at some point in her life (CBC interview). She states emphatically, "I want to see my friends, I want to see my family, I want do a little writing, if I can" (CBC interview).

And indeed, Shields continues to work, publishing two books in the first few months of 2001, with at least one more due her publisher by midyear. As she comments in *Dropped Threads*, "I thought for a while that serious illness had interrupted my chaptered life, but no, it is a chapter on its own. Living with illness requires new balancing skills. It changes everything, and I need to listen to it, attend to it and bring to it a stern new sense of housekeeping" *(Dropped Threads* 347). She concludes, "But I have time for this last exercise. All the time in the world" (347).

Carol Shields has undergone chemotherapy treatments yet again, most recently in Vancouver, in March and April of 2001. Characteristically thoughtful, eloquent, and gracious, she agreed to several telephone interviews prior to leaving for the hospital. When asked, she denied feeling nervous or uncomfortable about the treatment, "but I don't look forward to being in the hospital. I love to be home and in my own bed." Home again six days later, she continued her work on a new novel, inspired, as she is so often, by the kind of book that is missing from the market, the kind of book she would like to read but cannot find: it is a novel about work, about a writer, and one eminently well suited to the prize-winning author of *The Stone Diaries*. Shields sounds completely serious as she comments, "I love having this huge task waiting in the background."

2

The Novel

SYNOPSIS

The Stone Diaries, written in 1993, winner of the Canada Governor's Award in 1993, shortlisted for the Booker Prize in 1993, and winner of the Pulitzer Prize for Fiction in 1995, is the fictional autobiography of Daisy Goodwill Hoad Flett, a woman born in Canada and reared both in Manitoba and the United States. She lives from 1905 to the 1990s, the exact date of her death unknown. Artfully conceived and structured, the novel incorporates a family tree, photographs, recipes, grocery lists, letters, and numerous other techniques to convey a sense of Daisy and her family and friends. Most notable is the frequent switching back and forth between first and third person narrators so that on the surface a number of characters seem to be telling the story. In fact, Shields has emphasized that, whether in first person or third, all the voices are those of Daisy, half-orphaned daughter of an orphan who spends her life—through travels, marriage, children, and work—trying to come to terms with her true identity. "All those other voices," says Shields, "are filtered through Daisy—she's always imagining what other people think of her and, in the last chapter, she's still alive, thinking of the meatloaf, the hat, and so forth, imagining what's happening." The novel—a fictional biography or autobiography, depending on which person is speaking at any given moment—begins with Daisy's recounting of her mother and father's history and description of her own birth in 1905, then moves chronologically through various phases of her life: Her adoption by a neighbor, her childhood years in Winnipeg, her reunion with her father and their move to Indiana, her graduation from college, brief marriage and widowhood, return to Canada and remarriage, motherhood, career, and return to the United States, this time to a Florida retirement community. The novel ends on the eve of Daisy's death as Daisy continues to envision various perspectives of her life and behavior. The last words she ever speaks are "I am not at peace."

Although some readers find Daisy's story ultimately affirmative despite the sadness that imbues the book, Shields herself believes it's the "saddest book" she has ever written. "In fact," she recalls, "when I was signing a book for someone who wanted to give it to her grandmother, I felt like saying, 'Oh, no—don't give it to her—so many grandmothers haven't been able to claim their lives.'"

MAJOR CHARACTERS: THE GOODWILLS AND THE FLETTS

Mercy Stone Goodwill (1875–1905)

At such a far remove, it is difficult for readers to verify any information about Mercy. The line between fact and fiction must be even more blurred for Mercy than it is for her daughter. Nonetheless, we know that she was a foundling who lived at the Stonewall Orphan's Home and rose to a responsible level of employment within that establishment. Her ignorance of her own body was not atypical of the women of her day, so her surprise to learn that she is giving birth that sweltering summer day is almost surely genuine. Her pleasure in having a kitchen of her own and in creating dishes of her own must have been extremely meaningful to her, the birth of a baby interrupting the "small decencies and duties that steady her life: her needlework, her housekeeping, her skill with a flat iron, her preserves and pickles and fresh linens and the lamp chimneys she polishes every single morning."[11] Her death must have come as a shock equal to that of her pregnancy, but it had far-reaching and debilitating consequences for Daisy, the daughter who would be motherless from the moment of her birth. Even at the end of the novel, when Daisy is an old woman, we realize the influence a mother—even an absent mother—continues to wield, even if the daughter is unconscious of it: It is imperative that Daisy merge with Mercy before she dies and, in her imagination, she succeeds.

Cuyler Goodwill (1876–1955)

Cuyler is a good man, a perfect example of the way one can succeed through a combination of talent, effort, and luck. Coming as he does from the most unlikely of families (his parents are the unimaginative William Goodwill and Hannah Brody from Stonewall Township), he works, as does everyone he knows, with stone, at the quarry. And it is this skill with stone that leads him to the Stonewall Orphan's Home where he meets Mercy. His overwhelming love for Mercy produces Daisy, his overwhelming grief at her untimely death causes his shock and his abandonment of his infant daughter, and, finally, his love and grief inspire his creation of the Goodwill Tower to memorialize Mercy's death. Over time she recedes in his memory: With the splendid job opportunity in Indiana, he awakens to the fact that he has an eleven-year-old daughter, and together they embark on the American version of their lives. Cuyler enjoys phenomenal success in Indiana, rears Daisy to young womanhood, marries Maria Faraci in 1935—but remembers his young love for his first wife Mercy in the last scene as he lies dying.

Shields also uses him as an example of the phases or incarnations of an individual's life: "In his twenties he was a captive of Eros, in his thirties he belonged to God, and, still later, to Art. Now, in his fifties, he champions Commerce" (92)—and, in due time, he will revert to Eros, and then to Travel, and finally, to a cottage on a lake that possibly reminds him of earlier times and the blissful life with his first wife.

Daisy Goodwill Flett (1905–199?)

Daisy has been called Everywoman,[12] but in fact some critics debate the accuracy of such a term, for she is compelling, extraordinary and unique in many ways. Even though her voice and face are obscured (she is multivoiced, and the only character for whom we have no photo) and even though discrete parts of the novel concern her friends or family rather than herself, in the end it is Daisy whom we remember, Daisy whose unfulfilled life haunts us. Although her creator says that once in each chapter Daisy speaks in first person, "mostly, she is a baffled, seeking, third-person character, ever wandering through the construct that she calls her life story" (Hollenberg 6). Penelope Fitzgerald sees Daisy herself as a "closet Post-Modernist,"[13] reporting on her life by standing away from it as if she were an independent viewer.

Paradoxically, however, we keep returning to the fact that she is faceless, that we have no picture of her, and so we end with more questions than answers about Daisy's life, one that was simultaneously "empty and full, disconnected and connected, unstructured and structured."[14] Daisy rarely speaks. She becomes a hollow structure full of "dark voids and unbridgable gaps" (75), and one critic points out that she seems to spend her entire life sleepwalking.[15] In Winifred M. Mellor's words, "the erasure of Daisy from the text of her own life is an uncanny and chilling testament to the invisibility of women in the daily text of male-controlled existence."[16] Notably, we hear her voice only when she is with other women: her girl-friends (106, 130), Victoria (290) and Alice (323) (Mellor 106). None of her letters survives, and, as Barker's niece, it is not Daisy's own account but rather his male gaze and reluctant attraction to her that marks her adolescence. In fact, as she emerges from the dark-ness of the sickroom, the account is one of an awakening, but into darkness, not into brightness: Daisy knows with a disturbing finality that survival will require an effort of will and all the imagination she can muster. As if to emphasize this realization, her first and third person perspectives conflate permanently into the single seeking soul that Daisy will remain into old age (75).

If Daisy has a salvation and a passion, it is her writing, similar in effect to her mother Mercy's cooking, her Aunt Clarentine's garden-ing, and her great-niece Victoria's studies. Indeed, the only time she fights occurs when she loses her work, and the only time she feels in possession of her identity in old age occurs when she sees that the nurses have mistakenly used her maiden name on the hospital bracelet. If at the end we conclude that Daisy is an unreliable nar-rator, using only imagination to help her survive a life whose very core is despair, she seems very much like Thomas Hardy's Tess of the d'Urbervilles lying on her cold slab moments prior to death.

Carentine Barker Flett (1859–1916)

Although different from Mercy, she seems to echo a generational longing and loneliness. Like Mercy, she can neither fathom nor return the ardor of her husband: "She is a woman whose desires stand at the bottom of a cracked pitcher, waiting" (15). Daisy provides an alternate view, too, when she calls Clarentine "a woman half-crazed by menopause and loneliness" (37). She has befriended Mercy, hoping for an even closer friendship with the young woman whom, as she later tells Cuyler, she loved with all her heart (50). When Mercy dies, Clarentine sees the opportunity to care for the motherless baby, escape her unhappy marriage, and strike out, in a limited way, on her own. Moving to her son Barker's house in Winnipeg, she starts her own flower business, makes her own money, and provides Daisy with a better home than she would have had with her father at that time. As Daisy enters adolescence, Clarentine is killed in a freak accident. Her death sets in motion the next stage of Daisy's life: Barker moves to Ottawa, Cuyler is offered a job in Indiana, and Daisy leaves Canada to live with her father.

As Daisy matures, she understands the unusual heroism of Clarentine: "Yes, she had distorted and remade her own history, abandoning a husband and her wifely duties" (113), and even Barker admires her, thinking tenderly of his mother in the years following her death. On the eve of Daisy's marriage to Harold, Barker sends her as a wedding gift the wisely invested results of the sale of Clarentine's florist business, telling Daisy that Aunt Clarentine would have wanted her to have the money, "believing as she did that every woman, married or otherwise, must have a little money of her own. Pin money, she would have called it" (113). Clarentine dies amidst the sorts of coincidences that continue to intrigue Shields: Years later, we learn that the boy who caused Clarentine's death has become wealthy, and he creates the Clementine Flett Conservatory, a monument to her life and love of flowers.

Barker Flett (1883–1955)

Escaping his roots in Tyndall, Manitoba, Barker is poised for happiness with his position as a botany professor at Wesley College in Manitoba. Barker's love of botany, particularly the sensuous lady's-slipper, is illustrative of the way Shields has "scrambled" the metaphors of flower and stone. He is more aligned with his mother Clarentine and Daisy than with the rough-hewn men of stone from his youth. The appearance of his mother, who has left his father for good, bringing with her the infant Daisy Goodwill—and no money—alters Barker's peaceful plans for the future. To his credit, however, Barker supports his mother both psychologically and financially, despite the hardship they inject into his young life.

A gentleman in his quiet, scholarly way, he writes Cuyler Goodwill after his mother's death, tells him he is being transferred to Ottawa, and tacitly acknowledges his attraction to the young Daisy. His sense of obligation to her continues: On Daisy's marriage to Harold Hoad, Barker sends her a check for $10,000, a sum accrued from investments of Clarentine's profits from her flower business. He has kept all his letters to her and, in his way, has been in love with her all her life. When as a young widow Daisy finally visits Ottawa from Indiana, where Barker has become Director of Agricultural Research, she and Barker marry almost immediately.

Magnus Flett (1862–1978)

Although Clarentine was bored and unhappy with him, a man like the stone of his native Orkney Islands, he has his own problems, too, and Shields is at pains to delineate his perspective. He genuinely mourns Clarentine after she leaves, and her departure prompts him to begin reading novels. After his return to the Orkney Islands, he becomes famous as the man who can recite the entire novel *Jane Eyre* by heart. Because no one in his family cares whether he is alive or dead, we learn no more of him until Daisy finally locates him in an old age home in the Orkneys where he has reached the age of 115. Magnus also provides an opportunity for Shields to weave into her narrative a strand of immigrant history.

SETTING

Like so many of her other works, this novel shows Shields equally at home in both Canada and the United States; indeed, in a reversal of Shields's own situation, Daisy, born and reared in Canada until age fourteen, moves to the American midwest and marries an American. Then, however, like Shields, she moves to Canada and marries a Canadian, eventually returning to the United States to spend the rest of her days in Florida.

The first Canadian stage is set in Manitoba: Cuyler is from Stonewall Township, Mercy is from the Stonewall Orphans Home in Stonewall Township; Cuyler works in the Quarry and he and Mercy have a house in Tyndall, where Daisy is born. Magnus and Clarentine Flett live next door. When Clarentine Flett leaves with Daisy, they join her son Barker on Simcoe Street in Winnipeg.

When Daisy is eleven years old, a number of unexpected events occur: Clarentine dies, and both her "Uncle" Barker and her father Cuyler are offered posts that would involve relocating some distance away, Barker to Ottawa, Cuyler to Bloomington, Indiana, where Daisy's adolescence, college education, engagement, and marriage occur. She spends a few weeks in France during her ill-fated honeymoon, but with Harold's death she returns to Indiana where she lives with her father until she is thirty-one.

At that point she surprises her friends Fraidy and Beans with her uncharacteristically detailed itinerary to Niagara Falls, Callendar,

Toronto, and Ottawa. In the later city she marries Barker, raises all her children and, with Barker's death, writes Mrs. Green Thumb, her gardening column. Only after losing her job and recovering from her depression does she move to Sarasota, Florida, where she buys a condominium and maintains a balcony garden. From Sarasota she takes one more overseas trip, to the Orkney Islands, and then returns to Florida where eventually she moves to Sarasota Memorial Hospital and ultimately to the Canary Palms Rest Home where she dies in an unspecified year in the 1990s.

THEMES AND IDEAS

Carol Shields's novel bursts with provocative ideas, themes, and questions. At its very core is the question, how can we ever understand another person's life? Shields herself has said that "Daisy may be obsessed with stories, impressions, her need to exaggerate," but certainly my own obsession is biography." Who has the right to tell a life story? To what degree are we allowed to control our own stories? In this regard, the novel is about the role of the imagination and the degree to which it plays a central role in our lives. How does one convey silences and voicelessness, and how do they relate to the nature and uses of language itself? On one level this is, as Ida Sturino points out, also a novel about the "acquisition of language" (Sturino Internet 4): Cuyler Goodwill discovers language when making love to his wife, Daisy Flett through writing her gardening column, Magnus Flett through reading *Jane Eyre*, and Barker Flett becomes eloquent only when dying. Shields, however, though she always grounds her work in "a sophisticated understanding of current litcrit debates," claims she never permits her work to be engulfed by those issues (Hughes 40).

The novel contains a brilliant examination of the inner and outer self, and its author understands that "Certain behaviors are unclassifiable. Even fossils have some images superimposed on each other. But *humans* don't always fit neatly. We're products of so many conflicting impulses—that's always a chance that writers take, hoping that readers will feel the same way 'to get it'—and you hope you're right." She adds, "I don't think complexity is gendered; men are just as complicated as women," and Shields provides some finely tuned insights into the difficulties of all her characters. Yet she says that she was inspired to write this book about an ordinary middle class woman's life after hearing a young writer refer to the "blue-rinsed crowd."[17]

The novel also examines the issue of free will and chance, whether our lives are formed by conscious acts or by the accretion of numerous tiny accidents, coincidences, and unexpected turns of events. And, as in nearly all her books, she uses some of her characters to touch on the issue of immigration and the position of Canada in relation to the United States. Shields acknowledges that "[n]o one pays attention to Canada—I grew up in Illinois, and don't think I could even spell Saskatchewan." These are minor issues, however, compared to the central role of imagination in this tale, and to the role of women in Canada and the United States during the early part of the twentieth century.

TECHNIQUES

Carol Shields is a master at using traditional techniques in an experimental way. In the largest and most general sense, she creates this novel using biography and autobiography combined with fictional devices. As Jay Parini has noted, "The novel willfully smudges the already blurred distinctions between fact and fiction" (Parini 173). The genesis of the novel is instructive. Shields recalls, "I didn't have this all laid out; I took the structure from the old nineteenth-century biographies, and then the story came as I wrote. I started out to write a subversion of the old family saga, but then I realized it was about biography, autobiography, writing a life. And I was only into the second chapter when I knew that I would use photos and a family tree . . . the idea came quite early." Shields's postmodern approach is typified in the way she combines the traditional epistolary technique with seemingly random newspaper clippings, speeches, historical accounts, scientific jargon, definitions, photographs, recipes, conversations, obituaries, wedding announcements, telephone conversations, poems, grocery lists, and shopping memos.

Another notable way that Shields achieves her effects is through varied and often confusing points of view: "Brilliant ventriloquist that Shields is, we forget for pages at a time that Daisy is the only narrator of this tale; every utterance, every hard-edged interpretation, has her name on it."[18] Unlike the more traditional autobiographical narratives in which the narrator provides a sense of coherent design and structure, in this novel the numerous interruptive narrative voices prevent us from ascribing authority and "truth" to one voice. Shields also seems to suggest that identity cannot actually exist apart from these other voices and perceptions.

Shields has often gone on record as someone who really does not trust metaphor and symbol. In a recent clarification, she stated, "The symbolism of stones and flowers bind readers to a form of gender imagery, so I deliberately scrambled them. I'm not against metaphor *per se*, just what I might call 'conscious metaphors.' What's that saying . . . 'symbols are the fleas of literature'? The sort of symbols that the high school teacher would have us translate. It's the *conscious* use that I object to, not the unconscious."

As in all Shields's work, her technique pays specific artistic attention to the imagination and to its relation to the process of art itself: "Call it a dispensation of nature—a genetic burst that places a lyre in the throat, a bezel on the tongue" (84). And in Daisy's search for a way to tell her story, one can simultaneously see an equation of art and identity formation. When Daisy recovers from her measles, she understands clearly for the first time that "if she was going to hold on to her life at all, she would have to rescue it by a primary act of imagination, supplementing, modifying, summoning up the necessary connections . . . even dreaming a limestone tower into existence, getting the details wrong occasionally, exaggerating or lying outright, inventing letters or conversations of impossible gentility, or casting conjecture in a pretty light" (76–77). Daisy's insights into the central role of the imagination echo those of the writer herself, who observes that "[i]t's true that many of the comments about Daisy's process of trying to understand identity and character can be applied to art, too—art standing in for consciousness."

Shields is not concerned with history as central fact in *The Stone Diaries*, but says she enjoyed doing the research that enabled her to convey a sense of the eras she covers in the novel: "Although I didn't do very much intensive research for the book, I found I was discussing my work with everybody, and people were extremely helpful. A colleague found that the slang expression, 'I'll see you in church,' was first used in 1929. My children say I still say 'Oh boy,' and I know my mother says 'lickety split'!" The novel is peppered with such phrases as "lickety-split" (99, 157), "hunky-dorey" (145), "like a house afire," "like Gangbusters" (318), and with such popular song titles as "Keep the Home Fires Burning" (67), and "Ain't She Sweet" (89).

"Librarians," recalls Shields, "were wonderful in finding sources for me—originals of women's magazines, for instance—and leaving them open for me on the table where I did my writing. And I had a correspondent who helped me understand how it feels to be old. I wrote with a great sense of happiness, and in a very public way." Without ever losing focus on Daisy, the novel spans most of the twentieth century. The narrator briefly alludes to The Great War, World War II, the building of the Empire State Building (82), the

Great Depression, Lindbergh's transatlantic flight, the birth of Dionne quintuplets, the engagement of Prince Philip and Princess Elizabeth (182), Canadian immigration, such differing books as Betty Friedan's *The Feminine Mystique* and Catherine Parr Traill's *Wild Flowers of Canada*, and such movie stars as Esther Williams, Deborah Kerr, Barbara Stanwyk, and Greta Garbo.

Ultimately, like her creator, Daisy is an observer. Just as the protagonist of *Small Ceremonies* confesses, "I am a watcher. My own life will never be enough for me, . . ." Shields in her role as closely watchful observer gives veracity to *The Stone Diaries*.

TITLE

Although all readers naturally hope to interpret the title accurately, and numerous critics have done so quite persuasively, we should keep in mind that, as Shields says, "the title *The Stone Diaries* was not mine—it was created by committee at the New York publisher. I had a working title of 'Stone and Flower,' but that was too heavily symbolic, and it led too easily to gender stereotypes. I also thought of 'Daisy Goodwill: A Life,' and 'Monument.' But they preferred *The Stone Diaries*, and I've never felt completely comfortable with it. And it's not the first time a publisher has invented titles for my books." Shields notes that in her use of the metaphors of stone and flower, she deliberately "scrambled" them so that one would not ascribe stereotypical gender qualities to them. Thus Cuyler Goodwill and Magnus Flett, for example, are associated with stone, but Magnus' son Barker is a botanist by profession whose life work centers on a collection of lady's slippers, while Mercy Stone has nothing to do with flowers but is from Stonewall Orphanage, Stonewall Township, and is given Stone for a surname. When Cuyler builds the Goodwill Tower, he spends winter evenings carving flowers as well as animals on the stone pieces, and he does so in

Mercy's kitchen, scene of her food creations—and of Mercy's death and Daisy's birth.

The overly obvious, almost intrusive use of stone in this novel is notable. To cite just a few examples, Cuyler falls in love while resetting stone, his parents' adamantine clock chimes six o'clock at Daisy's birth, Cuyler is a stone cutter who earlier worked at Stonewall Quarries, and later in Indiana he works as a carver, builds a stone house, and makes money through his stone carving company. When Cuyler has a stone removed from his throat, he finds his voice and ability with words that Daisy inherits. Daisy is born in Stonewall Township, lives in Winnipeg, a city of limestone, and hears her father deliver her college graduation address on the permanence of stone. Her Aunt Clarentine is killed on a bank cornerstone possibly quarried by Magnus. Daisy's first husband Harold Hoad falls to his death on a stone pavement, she lives with her second husband Barker in a stone and brick house, on her visit to the Orkneys she stays at Grey Stones Hotel, and near the end of her life, she envisions herself and her mother as a blended stone effigy.

Numerous critics have suggested that many characters meet their deaths by stone. Conversely, it can signify solidity, progress, the American dream, the orderliness of life marked by milestones. Superficially, stone exudes solidity and permanence when compared with flowers—or diaries—which are fragile and evanescent, but ultimately, weathering and vandalism make even stone impermanent. Stone is also the medium of art for Cuyler Goodwill, and Shields states that limestone is particularly appealing in this regard because it was initially made of living plants—leaves and flowers—before hardening into its present state ("Life and Times"). Shields invented the tower, but notes, "I'm very interested in what the French call 'brute art,' created by insane people and prisoners—tomato soup towers, for instance—for no reason we can fathom, with no connection or relation to art as we know it."

Flowers, though less obtrusive than stone in this novel, are clearly intended to be central. The protagonist's name, of course, is Daisy. Her Aunt Clarentine walks away from a bad marriage in part by selling flowers; later she prospers through her florist business and, although she is killed when thrown against a stone wall, a monument is erected to her memory by the man who accidentally killed her; the monument is a conservatory in memory of her love for flowers. Clarentine's son Barker is, as mentioned, a botanist, and when Daisy takes over his horticultural column, she is reborn as Mrs. Green Thumb, a personally significant identity that, in her daughter Alice's opinion, causes Daisy to veer, "accidentally, into her own life" (237).

There is no such thing as the Stone Diaries nor is the narrative structured like a diary. Diaries and journals are mentioned sporadically throughout the novel. With her marriage to Barker, Daisy gives up keeping her diary and loses her travel journal. Her friend Fraidy Hoyt keeps a diary of all her lovers. Her daughter Alice burns her own old diaries. Daisy's voice is suggested by idea of diary, yet the "text itself strains against the genre of diary-writing by erasing Daisy Goodwill from the writing of her life directly after she is born" (Mellor 98). Ultimately, perhaps, the Stone Diaries, rather than applying to any one item, refers instead to this entire book, a collection of multivoiced entries about Daisy, to be sure, but also about others. If the Goodwill Tower and the Clarentine Flett Horticultural Conservatory are monuments to Mercy and Clarentine, Daisy's two mothers, then perhaps her own far-ranging narrative may be viewed as both a monument to her individual life, scarred and imperfect, and as a testament to her strength of character.

STRUCTURE

Although Shields has been innovative in the structure and composition of her novels (e.g., *Happenstance* and *The Box Garden*, where the husband and wife accounts are printed back to back), the skeleton of *The Stone Diaries* is borrowed directly from the nineteenth-century biographers; it begins with the chapter entitled "Birth, 1905" and ends with "Death." Shields has said that "Daisy may be obsessed with stories, impressions, her need to exaggerate—my obsession is biography," and as she began work, knowing that she would subvert the old-fashioned stories of several generations of families, she realized that she would also need to subvert the traditional structures of earlier biographies. Adding the family tree and the photographs is part of the subversive structure that she has invented for *The Stone Diaries*.

EPIGRAPH

With its lines from Judith Downing's "The Grandmother Cycle," this epigraph recalls Shields's frequent references, as in *Various Miracles*, to Emily Dickinson's line, "tell all the truth but tell it slant." In *The Stone Diaries* Shields shines an oblique spotlight on the issues of autobiography and women's lives. In Downing's line, "her life could be called a monument," appear the oblique references, "shaped in a slant of available light," to the stone monuments of the novel.

FAMILY TREE

The Family Tree extends from Clarentine Flett's father Hiram Barker, born in 1831, to Alice Flett's second marriage, to Nigel Spanner, in 1990. Many critics have noted that Daisy is nearly buried in the extensive family tree that precedes the first chapter, and when we do find her, we are none the wiser as to her death date; it reads simply "199?" Along with the photos, however, the family tree lends an air of both authenticity and postmodern playfulness.

Mercy is a unique and fascinating character whom Shields, through her narrator Daisy, portrays vividly and sensuously. Because of her orphanhood and her ignorance, she is a most sympathetic young woman as well. She is a complete creation of Carol Shields who says, "Mercy Stone was not based on a real person; I invented her. Still, I've always been fascinated by these articles on women who are surprised to learn they've been pregnant for months and months." Shields says that she "actually knew a middle class, middle-aged woman who didn't know she was pregnant until the very last moment." Mercy's ignorance follows what must have seemed to her a stroke of very good fortune: Cuyler falling in love with her. Her own inability to feel love has poisoned her, Daisy surmises, and she pretends pleasure in the sexual act "as women are encouraged to do," but she cannot comprehend her husband's "immense, unfathomable ardor . . . as he climbs on top of her each evening, a thundering let loose against the folded interior walls of her body" (7). That Daisy will feel the same way about her own husband Barker suggests not only her slanted perception of her parents' relationship, but also the minuscule differences between the two generations of husbands and wives.

Although Daisy's account makes clear that Mercy does not love Cuyler the way he loves her, she has been excellently trained at the orphanage, and felt fortunate to have her own house and kitchen and supplies so that she can create works of art in the form of recipes. The kitchen is Mercy's studio where, on the day of her death, she is fashioning a Malvern pudding for two: she has no idea, of course, that she is about to add a third party to the mix, and the shock doubtless contributes to her death. In the words of critic Marjorie Fee, the elevated, sensuous language and Daisy's recounting of her mother "making Malvern Pudding on a sticky summer day is one of the most sensual and striking in the novel, filled with images of heat, fruit, cream, flesh and sex."[19]

Commenting on Mercy's complete surprise at learning that she is not only pregnant but nine months pregnant, Shields observes, "These women are completely ignorant of the ways their bodies function, of course, but for their children, this is the ultimate act of total rejection. From a child's point of view, what could be worse than knowing that your mother didn't even realize she was going to give birth, much less plan for you and welcome you?"

Mercy delights in food. "Almost as heavenly as eating," remarks Daisy, "was the making—how she gloried in it! Every last body on this earth has a particular notion of paradise, and this was hers, standing in the murderously hot back kitchen of her own house, concocting and contriving" as she does with the Malvern pudding on the day of Daisy's birth. Years later, says Daisy, she understands clearly that her mother's talent is like that of an "artist" (2).

As Shields points out, if one looks at the photo of Mercy, she is not nearly so fat as Daisy describes her in the birth chapter. One need only compare a novel by Charles Dickens— David Copperfield, for example, with its opening line, "I am born"—to appreciate the postmodern coup Shields has achieved with the child's detailed view of her own birth. And it is noteworthy that the opening line contains a strong assertive naming of her mother (again, thinking back to a Dickens novel, Great Expectations, young Pip's mother is already dead and forever unknowable, her epitaph on her husband's tombstone reading merely "Also Georgiana, Wife of the Above"). Because Daisy has the need to flesh out a substantial mother, however, she imagines a larger than life version of Mercy.

A sensuous, memorable account, it also constitutes one of the few times Daisy speaks with authority and a sense of self, a time when she had potential, a time before her story had already determined the life she would lead. She has heard about "the old Jew" who finds

Mercy and calls Clarentine for help: "It's hard nowadays to talk about the old Jew. . . . The brain's got to be folded all the way back to the time when the words 'old Jew' could be said straight out" (19). As Clarentine and Abram Skutari run to Mercy's kitchen, "it is a temptation to rush to the bloodied bundle pushing out between my mother's legs, and to place my hand on my own beating heart, my flattened head and infant arms amid the mess of glistening pulp" (23). At this point we begin to realize Shields's strategy. In the midst of this chaotic scene of blood-drenched birth and death, Daisy asks, "Blood and ignorance, what can be shaped from blood and ignorance?—and the pulsing, mindless, leaking jelly of my own just-hatched flesh" to which she longs to bring some sort of order and "symmetry" (23). This is not only Daisy's task, but the writer's task in general: how does one make sense of a life and give it shape? As her parents' adamantine clock chimes six o'clock in the evening, Daisy has set the stage for the rest of her story: "My mouth is open, a wrinkled ring of thread, already seeking, demanding, and perhaps knowing at some unconscious level that that filament of matter we struggle to catch hold of at birth is going to be out of reach for me" (39). Yet it is Daisy's nature not to succumb, for she insists on claiming that final breath that her mother died giving to her (40).

CHILDHOOD, 1916

Daisy's childhood is passed with Clarentine and Barker at the house in Winnipeg, and its account is buttressed by a number of letters written by Clarentine to Cuyler and Barker to Magnus. The account is also laced with Daisy's humorous, imaginative speculations as to what Barker's women students think of him. A stoop-shouldered academic at thirty-three, the harried professor who has devoted his life thus far to a study of the western lady's slipper, he entrances his students with his eloquence and passion for his subject. Most of the other men in 1916 are off at war, and rumors abound as to why Barker has remained, the most probable and "true" cause being that he is the main support of his mother and eleven-year-old niece. He loves the lady's-slipper (Venus) and is happy to have put Tyndall behind him—but then along comes his mother with a neighbor's baby, and the war, which causes Wesley College Principal MacIntosh to ask Barker to study hybrid grains and to teach chemistry, physics, and zoology as well as botany.

We learn that Clarentine left Magnus carrying only a bag, the baby, and a bouquet of Michaelmas daisies that she would sell for cabfare once she reached Winnipeg. Shortly thereafter she named the baby Daisy. Some of the artifacts Clarentine mentions—the lock of baby hair, the photo of Daisy—tantalize because she is the only person in the novel for whom no photo, no letters, and no mementos survive. Cuyler faithfully sends Clarentine eight dollars a month, but Barker's letters reveal that Magnus refuses to send his wife a cent, so that Barker describes money as his "never-ending source of distress" (52).

Goodwill tower is erected and publicized that year, and Clarentine makes a small sum from the sale of her flowers, although the greenhouse was expensive. Cuyler has a sort of epiphany when he finds God in the form of a rainbow near the cemetery, "a radiant slice of paradise" appearing just as he stands next to Mercy's grave (57). He realizes that the monument of her gravestone is not nearly substantial enough, so he decides to build a tower of stones held together with gravity, without mortar. Like the American transcendentalists of the previous century, Cuyler looks at the rainbows, at "sun and rain, cloud and light, flower and stone—they are each so closely bound together, so almost prophetically joined, that he experiences a spasm of joy to find himself at the heart of such a holy convergence" (59). Shields is aware of her kinship to the transcendentalists and of her frequent employment of the word *transcend*: "I do use the word 'transcend'—we all do have states in which our senses seem to transcend ourselves, and we have a sense of all these moments. Everyone has these, but perhaps only poets express them." Cuyler comes to "believe that the earth's rough minerals are the signature of the spiritual, and as such can be assembled and shaped into praise and affirmation" (63). Like Mercy, he often works in the kitchen, and his art takes the form of carving the images of nature and various forms he has seen in *The Canadian Farmer's Almanac* or the Bible or *Eaton's Catalogue*.

Cuyler finishes the Goodwill Tower and then his marriage, his conversion, and his tower "seem no more than curious intersections in a life that is stretching itself forward" as he receives from the president of the Indiana Limestone Company of Bloomington, Indiana, an invitation to fill an expert carver job. The Tower has a "hollow core" (70) and at the bottom beneath a circle of weeds "lies a small gravestone" (70), perhaps a quiet reminder that, along with the growing acclaim for and prominence of Cuyler, both Mercy and Daisy are described with allusions to hollowness.

Despite the monument, Daisy suggests that "my father's love for my mother had been damaged" by her silence and thus it might be "difficult for him to love the child" (61). Daisy recovers from the measles and spends weeks in a dark room. She contracts bronchial pneumonia, and "since no one remembered to open the curtains or provide a light, the period of Daisy Goodwill's secondary illness was also spent in darkness. In addition, the blocked smell of dust and feather pillows imposed a kind of choking suffocation, the beginning of what was to be a lifelong allergy" (74). She awakens with a feeling of anxiety and need: "What she lacked was the kernel of authenticity, that precious interior core that everyone around her seemed to possess." All this converges in the "on me, on Daisy Goodwill and emptied her out" sentence. "Her autobiography, if such a thing were imaginable, would be, if such a thing were ever to be written, an assemblage of dark voids and unbridgable gaps" (75–76). As she understands that this darkened room was where she would continue to live her life, "blinded, throttled, erased from the record of her own existence," she sees clearly that the only way to hold onto her life would be "to rescue it by a primary act of imagination, supplementing, modifying . . . getting the details wrong occasionally, exaggerating or lying outright, inventing letters or conversations of impossible gentility, or casting conjecture in a pretty light" (76–77). For instance, while Aunt Clarentine lies in a coma before dying from her accident, Daisy floats her to heaven on a bed of pansies "and, at the same time, translated her uncle's long brooding sexual stare, for that was what it was, into an attack of indigestion" (77). In these instances the child survives by denying and transforming the unpalatable realities of death and sex.

Then Clarentine is suddenly hit by a cyclist—Valdi Goodmansen (who bought the bicycle from Abram Skutari)—and dies, Barker relocates to Ottawa, and Cuyler accepts the invitation to work and live in Indiana. Daisy "willed herself to be strong" and this ability is key to her survival. She will never be completely happy, but neither will she be suicidal. And on the day her father comes to meet her and take her with him, she actually feels happy and remembers all the details of the meeting.

MARRIAGE, 1927

Opening with newspaper clippings of Miss Daisy Goodwill's engagement to Mr. Harold A. Hoad, this chapter alludes briefly to the events of Daisy's life in the eleven years since she left Winnipeg: she has graduated from Tudor Hall and Long College for Women, and she will be a June bride with all the ceremony of teas and Quarry Club dinners. Her father Cuyler's success is apparent, as is his surprising fame for eloquence: he believes, says Daisy as narrator, that his two-year marriage to Mercy is the cause of his "silver tongue," but Daisy herself believes he found it during his Manitoba rainbow conversion, in the cadences of the King James Bible, in his many interviews with journalists seeking information about the Goodwill Tower—or on the train trip from Winnipeg to Bloomington, when he "talked and talked and talked" (87) all the way through North Dakota and Minnesota and Wisconsin. We have only a passing sense of the pain Daisy must have endured, the trepidation she must have felt as she set out for a new country with "a parent who had surrendered her to the care of others when she was barely two months old" (90). From her perspective, he gave her talk rather than comfort, and from his, he chattered incessantly to try to fill in the gaps that he knew he could never, ever "pay back" (91).

We learn, too, about the process of "reverse immigration." Magnus Flett, for example, his wife having left him and his children having more or less ignored him, returns to his native Orkney Islands carrying only his wife's goodbye note, a few photographs, and four books: *Struggle for a Heart*, by Laura Jean Libby; *What Gold Cannot Buy*, by Mrs. Alexander; *At the World's Mercy*, by Florence Warden; and *Jane Eyre*, by Charlotte Bronte—his favorite (100). Shields has said that "Clarentine's novels (that Magnus later reads) actually existed. I found them in an old mail order catalogue from that period. It was useful to dip into it and add period flavor to the book—that's where, for example, I learned the cost of a wedding ring." In any case, Magnus's love for Clarentine is similar to young Cuyler's for Mercy; too late he learns the words of love he could have spoken to her before she ran away, but at least he has now found a love of words and of good writing.

Mrs. Hoad invites Daisy to a luncheon during which she imparts to her all the advice she believes would be useful to Daisy—one should say "death" rather than "passing away," she might try Venitian Velva Liquid for her skin, and never wear white shoes after Labor

Day. Some of it, however, is also clearly prejudiced toward her son Harold. For instance, Daisy should never let her college education "impinge on normal marital harmony" by parading her knowledge in front of Harold (who has been expelled from college, although his mother refuses to admit it), and Daisy should feed him Grape-Nuts for breakfast to make sure he has regular bowel movements. Although the interview (it does not sound like an intimate or cozy luncheon) sounds harsh, Shields says that Daisy's account of her mother-in-law is hyperbolic, just as is her account of her mother Mercy: "Daisy has exaggerated that scene, and made it into a story. Likewise with the obesity of her mother . . . if you look at the picture you see she's not nearly so fat as Daisy makes her sound." And referring to the subjects in the conversation, Shields vouches for their accuracy: "A lot of that advice I got in the 1950s . . . it was part of the economy, how do you make yourself a valuable wife? As a newlywed I asked my mother, 'how do you wash a blanket?' and my mother wrote out the instructions very seriously."

The most satisfying part of Daisy's life is her friendship with Fraidy and Beans, Elfreda Hoyt and Labina Anthony. Fraidy has traveled to Europe, eaten artichokes in a French bistro, viewed a young naked male model in an Italian art class, and instructed Daisy and Beans in the "highly sexed" and creative ways of the French, assuring them that oral intercourse is "perfectly natural" and that, after all, "they're not half as puritanical as we are in America" (107). Beans and Daisy exhibit varying degrees of horror and nausea at this illicit information, and then burst into gales of laughter: "Stop making me laugh," says Beans, "or I'll split my gee-dee seams open." Fraidy adds, "And I'm going to wet my gee-dee underpants" (107). This laughter, Daisy informs us, has "been going on forever," since their earliest school years together, through their pledging the same sorority—and when Daisy pauses to think about her honeymoon, "she always somehow imagines that Fraidy and Beans will be there

too, standing right next to her and whooping and laughing and rack-
eting around like crazy" (108). A somber chill descends as she realizes that, to the contrary, she'll be all alone with her new husband.

Harold A. Hoad has his own problems that, in typical naive fashion, Daisy believes she can alleviate. She cannot, of course; Harold
suspects that his mother has lied to him about the reasons for his
father's suicide, knows the rumors of his father's womanizing and
financial improprieties, and has been a full fledged alcoholic for
years. A few days before their wedding while walking together in the
public gardens, he swings a willow wand, lopping the heads off
numerous flowers and—in a perhaps suspiciously Freudian way—
Daisy says, "Don't do that with your stick." He continues to decapi-
tate flowers until she finally succeeds in stopping him. The fact is
that, gruesome as his honeymoon death is, it probably saved Daisy a
lifetime of grief. She is unable to stop him from drinking on their
honeymoon trip to France; indeed, "he almost groans with the pleasure of what he is hearing, his darling scolding bride who is bent so
sweetly on reform" (118). In the quiet Alpine town of Corps, Daisy
lies on her back on the bed while the drunken Harold tosses cen-
times to the children gathered below. Daisy has a premonition of
tragedy, sneezes loudly in allergic reaction to the hotel feather pillows, and then "hears a bang, a crashing sound like a melon split-
ting, a wet injurious noise" as Harold falls to his death (119–20).
Although it is never clear whether the sneeze startled Harold
enough to contribute to his fall, it is the only item in her later
recounting that Daisy omits.

LOVE, 1936

It probably has escaped no one's notice that the chapter on love follows rather than precedes the chapter on marriage. In fact, nine long
years pass while Daisy lives at home with her father, feeling helpless

in the face of the story of her tragic honeymoon, a story that she cannot move beyond, a story that "marches ahead of her." She sees the story in gendered terms: "Men, it seemed to me in those days, were uniquely honored by the stories that erupted in their lives, whereas women were more likely to be smothered by theirs" (121). In a narrative move that has become typical of her in this novel, Daisy then switches from the first person to the third, describing her thirty-one-year-old self as "she who's still living in the hurt of her first story, a mother dead of childbirth, and then a ghastly second chapter, a husband killed on his honeymoon" (122).

In an abrupt reversal, however, in an apt illustration of Shields's postmodernism, Daisy addresses the reader directly: "You might like to believe that Daisy has no gaiety left in her, but this is not true, since she lives outside her story as well as inside" (123). She tells us frankly that she willingly relinquished any claims on the Hoad fortune; and that ironically, just as Aunt Clarentine's florist business had prospered during the "bad old days" of the Great War, Cuyler Goodwill's stone carving art is thriving in the midst of the Great Depression (127). She has renewed her friendship with Fraidy and Beans (who know that she is still a virgin—the only one of them now, since Beans is married and Fraidy has been experimenting with sex). Prompted in part by her father's recent marriage to Maria, a middle-aged Italian woman whom he adores, Daisy surprises herself by planning a two-week trip to Niagara Falls and Canada that she regards as "a kind of mythic journey" in which "something might happen to me" (132).

And happen it does. She cherishes for years the memories of the Niagara Falls visit and the amusing New Yorker who makes her laugh; she feels indignant on viewing the young Dionne quintuplets in Callander, Ontario; the bank president patronizes her and the vice president propositions her when she delivers her father's blueprints to their bank in Toronto. When she reaches Ottawa and

Barker—who has written her 132 letters since she left twenty-two years ago—meets her train, the inevitable "something" occurs. He has cherished her memory for over two decades, actually letting her creep into his classification of the natural world: "She sits far out at the end of one of the branches, laughing, calling to him" (143). Although none of her letters to him has survived, Daisy has saved every single one of his to her. As the train nears the station, Daisy likens herself to Barbara Stanwyck in the *Woman in Red*, hoping to present a Garbo-like sprightliness as she shakes out her red-gold hair. If Barker is rumored to be homosexual, she is on the verge of eccentricity and middle-age, stuck in those inescapable stories of her life.

It is here that she confesses most fully to her willful dickering with truth and imagination, the writerly as well as the autobiographical paintbrush. It is here, too, that Shields tips her postmodern hand most fully. Daisy "has trouble with getting things straight" and would let "you" believe that hers had been a "golden childhood" (148). "Well, childhood is what anyone wants to remember of it," she says, as if to inquire, "what's wrong with this?" Daisy's unreliability is further attested to when she asks the reader, what mother-in-law could have been as terrible as Daisy makes Mrs. Hoad? And then she delivers perhaps the best-known line of the entire novel: "Still, hers is the only account there is, written on air, written with imagination's invisible ink" (149). It is Daisy's imaginative tellings of her life story that help illuminate the writer's task and the writer's methods—the creativity, the invention, the addition and subtraction. What else, indeed, but imagination?

As the train nears the station, Daisy pens what will be the last line she will ever write in her travel journal: "In one hour I will be there," she writes, underscoring the word "there" three times (150). Certainly she is powerless, womanly, soft, awaiting an "accident of fortune"—but she is also the agent of this trip, and has done as much as possible to will the "something" to happen (150). On her arrival,

Barker does not disappoint: "his blood is on fire" and he embraces her; they marry quickly and quietly. The chapter ends with the wishes and thoughts of people from the Canadian Prime Minister to Cuyler to Beans and Fraidy. Not surprisingly, Daisy's personal thoughts are lost: she chooses to stop keeping a personal diary, and her travel journal is last seen on the train. She comments only that she has now departed the province of girlhood.

MOTHERHOOD, 1947

The motherhood chapter is, interestingly, neither longer nor shorter than any of the other chapters of Daisy's life. It is divided into ten sections: *Suppertime, Alice, Warren, Joan, Mrs. Flett's Niece, A Letter Folded in Mrs. Flett's Drawer, Mrs. Flett's Aged Father, Mrs. Flett's Old School Friend, Mrs. Flett's Intimate Relations with Her Husband,* and *Mrs. Flett's House and Garden,* the entire chapter bisected by eight pages from the Flett family photo album. The structure seems to replicate the fragmentation of the motherhood phase of Daisy's life. Shields has commented, "I remember my mother always signing herself Mrs. Robert E. Warner—it's hard now to believe that women used to call each other Mrs. so-and-so," as if they did not even have first names.

The "Suppertime" section takes place on a hot July day and serves to introduce the three children—Alice, nine, Warren, seven, and Joan, five—and Mr. Mannerly, whom Daisy affectionately refers to several times throughout the novel. Mr. Mannerly helps with the extensive garden that Daisy maintains. Because of the tremendous heat that day, she fixes a cold supper and uses the Frigidaire to keep the jellied meatloaf cold. Daisy "fixes herself up" each evening before Barker returns home, looking "straight from the Oxydol ads," or at least this is the way her son Warren sees her (160). When Barker arrives home we learn that he is just months shy of his sixty-fifth birthday and will be forced to retire from the Directorship of the Agricultural Research Institute. He plans to work on his lady's-slipper collection, write a weekly horticulture column for the Ottawa *Recorder*, and publish a few academic articles. "How blessed the members of the Flett family are, never mind their disparate ages, their hidden thoughts, and the fact that they have little in common," says the narrator just before Barker and Daisy—pointedly referred to as Mr. and Mrs. Barker Flett—settle into their double bed, he with *The Botanical Journal* and she with *Better Homes and Gardens*. As Barker falls asleep, Daisy tells us that he has come to believe that love is "just a word trying to remember another word," sounding very much like William Faulkner's Addie Bundren in *As I Lay Dying*, who believes that love is "just another word to fill a lack." The name Daisy is never used in this section, for she is not Daisy to any of her family.

In the next scene Daisy explains sexual intercourse to Alice, who has already heard vulgar and erroneous versions from Billy Raabe down the street. On the part of both mother and daughter, Shields has captured perfectly the era's discomfort with sexual matters. Daisy looks at her cuticles and Alice knows that the "cloudless summer day has been spoiled. Nothing will ever be the same," recalling the way her mother dresses in the closet, pulling on girdle and stockings (167). Alice understands that she must not tell her brother and sister, not yet, and she appreciates her love for them and their unsullied innocence.

The next section centers on Daisy and Barker's son Warren. Because he is in the questioning phase, Warren loves to hear the answers to his queries about his birth, establishing the certainty of his identity. He knows he is a war baby, born "in the early days of the war," (169) and he thinks of himself and his sisters joined like paper dolls, himself always in the middle. He feels good except for the empty spot inside that knows the war is over, and the disquieting thought that his parents might have another baby. Daisy, her bobby pins winking in the light, tells him with notable seriousness that she and his father are too old to have more babies.

In her section, Joan, the youngest child, born in the middle of the war, has no exchanges with her mother the way her siblings do. Kissing her goodnight, her mother has no idea that little Joan's head is crammed full of secrets: "Already, at the age of five, Joan understands that she is destined to live two lives, one existence that is visible to those around her and another that blooms secretly inside her head" (172). She has learned to skip, bringing control into her life, and she knows a place where she can roll down the hill whenever she likes. She has complete self-confidence in her powers to achieve whatever she chooses.

The "Mrs. Flett's Niece" section shows a certain concern with propriety that although understandable, illuminates a less admirable aspect of Daisy's relationships that has not previously surfaced. Suddenly, with no warning, a niece of Andrew Flett—Barker's brother, a Baptist minister who constantly writes asking for money—appears unannounced on her way home from London, where she has been stationed as a WREN during the war. The children are mesmerized by her prettiness, her wit, her sense of humor, her forwardness, her use of slang, and her proximity to death, all of which fascinating topics disturb Mrs. Flett, who finds her too pert and lacking discrimination in the stories she tells the children. Mrs. Flett interrupts Beverly's war stories to ask her what time her train leaves so that they can take her to the station on time. She does not use the word, but in those days, the Mrs. Fletts would have considered Beverly vulgar or commonplace. In response to Alice's breathless compliments for Beverly, Mrs. Flett responds by rolling her eyes, sighing, and saying that she has "plenty of oomph" (178). Alice can read her mother's sigh and knows that in her own response to Cousin Beverly she is missing an element that her mother sees with complete clarity.

The following section concerns a letter from Fan Flett, Beverly's mother, in which she upbraids Daisy for her rude treatment of Beverly. Fan accuses Daisy of hustling Beverly out the door and failing to ask this niece whom she had never met and who had served her country to spend the night.

The "Mrs. Flett's Aged Father" section is an update on Cuyler Goodwill, who is now seventy years old. He and Maria have moved from their large Bloomington house into a cottage on Lemon Lake, Indiana, where she can grow a large vegetable garden and he can work on his latest project. Since he and Maria have returned from their cruise on the Nile, Cuyler has determined to return to his work with stone: this time, he plans on building a pyramid whose exterior will be made of pure white Indiana limestone. "He's obsessed," remarks Daisy, but she says so quite happily, believing as she does that "old people are better off obsessed than emptied out" (181). The tower is an ambitious project of two million tiny pieces of stone from around the world. In the center, buried under the foundation, Cuyler has constructed a time capsule to which Alice, Joan, and Warren, his three grandchildren, have already contributed artifacts: a local newspaper headline announcing the engagement of Princess Elizabeth and Prince Philip, a two-penny stamp bearing the likeness of King George VI, and a maple leaf. Maria has added fennel seeds—and Cuyler, "that eccentric old fool, has added, at the last minute, the wedding ring that belonged to his first wife" (182).

He had always intended to give the ring to Daisy in memory of the mother she never knew—and clearly he should have done so; it would have meant the world to her. In the past he has actually mentioned the ring to Daisy, promising to give it to her one day. But now "he has lost his way in life" and changes his mind; Daisy has no idea that he is burying the ring forever out of her reach, thoughtlessly confiscating his only daughter's sole inheritance. The action typifies the familiar Shields theme of happenstance, of the lack of certainty that things will turn out as one had hoped or planned.

In the next section, "Mrs. Flett's Old School Friend," the narrator calls the protagonist "Daisy" rather than "Mrs. Flett," for the only time in the "Motherhood" chapter of the novel. In this short but compact section we are offered two versions of Fraidy Hoyt's trip to Ottawa in August, 1947. In the first, Fraidy believes that Daisy has everything that she, Fraidy, lacks: "a distinguished husband and a large well-managed house and three beautiful children," whereas Fraidy has a dull job and no husband and is "missing out on this business of being a woman" (184). In the second version, however, Fraidy pities Daisy for letting herself gain weight, turn respectable, lose interest in her appearance, and put up with all the hypocrisy that family life entails: "What's left to say? I see you're still breathing, Daisy. I see you're still dusting that nose of yours with Woodbury Face Powder. . . . I believe your life is still going along, it's still happening to you, isn't it? Well, well" (184-185). The reader has the uncomfortable suspicion that the second version is rather more accurate than the first—or, at least, that only a combination of the two could truthfully portray Daisy's situation.

The next section is entitled "Mrs. Flett's Intimate Relations with Her Husband." In her sincere wish to be a good wife and mother, Daisy reads all the proper magazines of the era: *Good Housekeeping, McCall's* and *The Canadian Home Companion.* Tucked in among the recipes and advertisements she occasionally finds advice for "sexual problems." For example, because the wife never knows when her husband will desire sex, each night she should prepare herself for the event, inserting the diaphragm despite its repellent "yellow look of decay and the cold, sick-smelling jelly" that must be smeared around the edges (186). On this particular autumn evening, when Barker is due back from a trip to Winnipeg, Daisy thinks of the words she has read: "Try to make your husband believe that you are always ready for his entreaties, even though his actual lovemaking may be sporadic and unpredictable," and "The wearing of pajamas has driven many a man to seek affection elsewhere" (186). Shields has captured the essence of the women's magazines of the era. When asked if these are actual quotations, Shields answers, "One or two bits of advice actually come from a woman's magazine of the period, but many of them I invented—based, of course, on the tone and gist of the advice on 'conjugal responsibilities.' My own favorite is, 'You can say no to the invitation, but not too often!'"

One of the most striking aspects of this section is the way Shields apparently tries to portray Daisy's feelings with realistic detail and a sense of honesty and balance. She has been married eleven years and has known Barker all her life; she knows him well and thinks of him with affection. At the moment, for instance, she knows that he worries about having to retire, about an increased distance between himself and his brothers Andrew and Simon, and about his estrangement from his father Magnus: if it is too late for a reunion, Barker could at least learn whether or not he is still alive. Daisy, a symbol of otherness herself, feels sympathy for Magnus, and wonders if he really deserved such "punishment" (187).

Daisy is having one of the moments that Shields has spoken of as her "moment of clarity" in each chapter. Here she lies on her back, feeling the familiar gusts of grief that she occasionally allows herself. The past is always a part of the present, but she feels it especially deeply tonight, as Barker attends the ceremony honoring his mother Clarentine. Valdi Goodmansen, the millionaire meatpacker and financier, was the boy who hit and killed Clarentine with his bicycle, and he has never completely recovered from the tragedy. Tonight, always knowing that Clarentine loved flowers, he dedicates the new Clarentine Flett Horticultural Conservatory in her memory.

At this moment, however, Daisy is thinking not so much of her dear adopted mother Aunt Clarentine as of her own mother Mercy.

She owns only a fuzzy wedding photo and a small foreign coin placed on her head moments after her birth, nothing that her mother had actually touched. She has yearned for the wedding ring of which her father Cuyler has spoken, but has never received it, and "she feels the loss of that ring, the loss, in fact, of any connection in the world." Daisy suffers from the illness called "orphanhood . . . and here she lies, stranded, genderless, ageless, alone" (189). Weeping in the darkened bedroom, Daisy feels the full force of her loneliness. And yet, as always, Daisy has a particular power that enables her to see the world with clarity just at the moment she most needs it: "she possesses, as a compensatory gift, the startling ability to draft alternate versions" as she sees through the "narrative maze" to her children's secrets, her father's eccentricities, Fraidy's mingled envy and contempt. Tonight Daisy even feels a link with her mother, as if she herself has given birth to Mercy, rather than the reverse.

Having mastered the bout of unhappiness that comes over her like a migraine headache, Daisy returns to the present, considers the "debris" of her married life, and projects ahead to the next hour when Barker will make love to her—"That men and women should be bound to each other in this way! How badly reality is organized"—and he will tell her to sleep tight and forgive him for his sexual needs.

The chapter concludes not with the examination of the marital relationship but with that of "Mrs. Flett's House and Garden." Although her Ottawa house at 583 The Driveway is, like the rest of the world, recovering from wartime shortages and postwar fatigue, Daisy does not care much about the house at all. Instead, she lives for, is known for and sustained by her beautiful, originally conceived garden, with its artistically arranged plantings admired by all who encounter them. "This garden of Mrs. Flett's is lush, grand, and intimate—English in its charm, French in its orderliness, Japanese in its economy—but there is something, too . . . that is full of grave intelligence and even, you might say, a kind of wit" (195). It is her Eden, her paradise, "her dearest child"—and she loves its greenness and its purity and its secrets and, perhaps most of all, its complete detachment from her own history and longings. This section, more than any other, prepares us for the next chapter entitled "Work." It also ties Daisy even more closely to her mother Mercy, who felt that cooking was her paradise, and her Aunt Clarentine, whose garden was her Eden.

PHOTOS

The idea to use photos came to Shields "quite early." She recalls, "I was only into the second chapter when I knew that I would use photos and a family tree." The photo section, consisting of eight pages, appears right in the middle of the book, appropriately enough in the already multi-fragmented "Motherhood" chapter. It begins with a full-page picture of Cuyler and Mercy Goodwill dated 1902, and is followed by the splendid full-page Ladies Rhythm and Movement Club. The smaller ones on the proceeding two pages include Cuyler's mother, Hannah Goodwill; Bessie McGordon, the Matron of Stonewall Orphan's Home and therefore a sort of foster mother to Mercy Stone; the enticing one of Aunt Clarentine in 1916 (in stark contrast to another, presumably taken during her unhappy marriage to Magnus Flett); and Barker as a young man. The next two pages show photos of Mrs. Arthur Hoad and a baby picture of young Harold, a sedate photo of Beans Anthony and two vivacious pictures (one an artist's sketch) of Fraidy Hoyt, followed by photos of Warren and Victoria Flett as small children. On the next page we see a picture of the Flett house at 583 The Driveway in Ottawa, a group shot of Mr. and Mrs. Mannerly, the housekeeper and gardener, their son Angus, along with Beverly, Warren and Alice, and a separate baby picture of Alice. The last two pages show Daisy's grandchildren and great-great niece and nephew.

The inclusion of the photos constitutes a brilliantly provocative addition to the novel. On one level, the pictures represent the more playful side of postmodernity: will Shields's readers enter the game of ascribing photos of "real" people to the novel's "fictional" characters? On another, they give the lie to some of the narrator's descriptions: When Mrs. Hoad gives her prospective daughter-in-law advice, for example, as Shields readily points out, "Daisy has exaggerated that scene, and made it into a story." On still another, they emphasize the arbitrariness of life writing: who gets to write it? how much of it is true? and how much blends and blurs the line between fact and fiction?

One of the photos most frequently remarked on is that of the Ladies Rhythm and Movement Club, the one Magnus takes with him to prove that Clarentine was happy sometimes, and he consoles himself with this thought: "She cannot have been oppressed and ill-used twenty-four hours a day for twenty-five long years" (98). When asked about that photo, Shields replies in a similar way: "I liked the picture because it shows that women did get out of the kitchen, they did have a physical life, did join Snowshoe Clubs, weren't beaten twenty-four hours a day!" She notes that she found the picture in a little museum and, much to her delight, after the book was published, "four of the descendants of those women have contacted me."

Shields's editor helped her find some of the other photos, gathering them from museums, antique stores and a Parisian postcard market. The last two pages actually contain childhood pictures of Carol Shields's own children.[20]

WORK, 1955–1964

The chapter on work opens with Barker's death—of a malignant brain tumor that was not discovered until very late. The sadness and poignancy of his feelings for Daisy and his marriage are eloquently portrayed in the letter he writes to her following the news that he is dying. After offering her the lady's-slipper collection to sell so that she might travel, he points out that over the years it has been the only subject of real disagreement between them. Recalling Daisy's repugnant feelings for the flower, with its "long gloomy (as you claimed) stem and pouch-shaped lip which you declared to be grotesque . . . I pointed out. . . the lip's functional cunning, that an insect might enter therein easily but escape only with difficulty. Well, so our discussions have run over these many years, my pedagogical voice pressing heavily on all that was light and fanciful" (198). More significantly, perhaps, he notes that he and Daisy rarely used the word "love" (198), and he regrets this fact, hoping that their children will be more forthcoming and use the word "extravagantly" (199). He then turns a 1950s plastic apron into a romantic metaphor as he recollects the first harbinger of his death, the dreadful headache that Daisy tried to soothe for him: "I loved you terribly at that moment. The crackling of your apron against my body seemed like an operatic response to the longings which even then I felt. It was like something whispering at us to hurry, to stop wasting time, and I would like to have danced with you through the back door, out into the garden, down the street, over the line of the horizon. Oh, my dear. I thought we would have more time" (199). He signs the letter "Your loving Barker."

Perhaps nowhere else does Shields so clearly point out the complexity of human feeling. She manages to convey the loss of a husband of twenty years who, even then, pays romantic tribute to the woman he has loved since her girlhood, but then, through more letters, she shows Daisy's grasp of the other perspectives on her loss: Fraidy reminds her that she has many years left to enjoy, and, through the letters of Jay Dudley, editor of the *Ottawa Recorder*, we see that Daisy is able to accept a tribute to her husband and graciously respond, yet at the same time suggest that she might write the article on tulips he would have written were he still alive.

Reinventing herself as Mrs. Green Thumb, Daisy talks herself into a job that lasts for about nine years.

Of course Daisy would never have found a job had Barker not died. He leaves her in good shape financially, so when Dudley invites her to a ceremony celebrating Barker's contributions, under the name of Mr. Green Thumb, to the paper's horticultural column Daisy has no need to work. Nonetheless it is ironic that his death provides the vacancy for her to fill, while the lady's-slipper collection that he believed worth a good bit of money is, ironically, faintly disparaged by his colleague at Boston University, who finds it less than complete and slightly substandard in its preservation.

As Mrs. Green Thumb, Daisy proves herself a born writer. Her love for and knowledge of gardening, combined with the writing talent she demonstrated in college (as even Warren, astonished, and Alice, somewhat patronizingly, grant her) secure her an admiring and loyal readership. The entire chapter— the shortest of all—is epistolary in technique, conveying the changes in Daisy and her family during the nine years following Barker's death. Cuyler dies in 1955, the same year as Barker, in a moving scene in which his mind—with some significant memory lapses—ranges over his entire life while his body lies helplessly paralyzed from the stroke that kills him shortly afterward. He struggles in his efforts to recall the name of his first wife, but finally and surely to the delight of most readers, remembers the word "Mercy." Beans, who married in 1927, the same year Daisy married Harold Hoad, loses her husband Dick to a "little lady friend." Fraidy marries a man named Mel. Alice begins her first year at Smith College, then marries and moves to England. And Daisy invites Cousin Beverly, whom she had snubbed on her return from the War, to live permanently with her. Beverly, divorced from her alcoholic husband Jerry Davenport, has become pregnant after a very brief liaison with a Leonard Mazurkiewich. She never sees him again, but she does give birth to Daisy's great niece Victoria

Louise, who—after some initial resistance from Daisy's children—
becomes a loved and valued family member. Beverly helps with the
household and types all of Daisy's articles. Daisy actually overcomes
her fear of flying to spend time with Alice, who seems to suffer more
overtly than her siblings from her father's death. Warren begins his
first year at Hanover College. His mother enters into a romance with
Jay Dudley and receives at least twenty admiring letters a week from
readers of her gardening column.

Daisy also finds time for getaway vacations with Fraidy and
Beans, during which absences Pinky Fulham, another *Recorder*
columnist, fills in for her. He has wanted her column for himself for
years, but it is only when Jay wishes to disentangle himself from his
relationship with Daisy (he desperately fears marriage) that he
makes the decision to give the column permanently to Pinky, cal-
lously firing Daisy over the telephone. Daisy has no voice of her own
during any of this traumatic time (as usual, her correspondence has
disappeared), but we learn, chiefly from the letters written by Pinky
and Jay, that she fights harder to retain this job than she has ever
fought for anything in her life. The two men keep telling her not to
take the decision "personally," and profess astonishment at Daisy's
utter devastation when she learns that she is no longer Mrs. Green
Thumb. The chapter ends with an awful silence, punctuated by letters from Fraidy and Alice asking why Daisy has stopped writing.

SORROW, 1965

"1965 was the year Mrs. Flett fell into a profound depression"
(229). So writes Daisy about herself from the distance not only of
third person and the formality of "Mrs. Flett," but also from the perspectives of nine additional friends and family members. Once
again, as in the chapter entitled "Motherhood," the viewpoints
make the chapter on "Sorrow" seem fragmented and disjointed—

exactly the situation in which Daisy finds herself. That the chapter begins and ends with Daisy, despite the use of third person most of the time, suggests that she has more control over her period of depression than one would think.

In the opening of the chapter, Daisy asks, what is the source of this depression? She acknowledges her unattractiveness during this time, but repudiates the idea that either menopause (she is fifty-nine) or delayed mourning is the cause. Stating frankly that she rarely thinks back to her husband or their twenty years of marriage, she insists that her depression stems "from some mysterious suffering core which those around her can only register and weigh and speculate about" (230). The sections that follow include "theories" about her depression from nine family members and friends, and ends with Daisy's own.

Alice's theory actually has very little to do with her mother. Not that she is unsympathetic: Alice has left her husband in charge of the children in England and has flown home to be with her mother. But she believes that one can reinvent oneself, and in fact, has done exactly that: she recalls returning home from college one summer and deciding to become a different person—to grow kind, to burn her old diaries and letters, and, in short, to grow up. Then, cataloguing the myriad changes in the house after her father's death, Alice expresses surprise that, far from being engulfed by all the tragedy, her mother had come "bobbing to the surface, her round face turned upward to the sunlight, happy" (238). And when she became Mrs. Green Thumb—presto!—"Her old self slipped off her like an oversized jacket" (239). Alice describes Daisy's total absorption in her job and the attendant happiness of being a well-known local personage who loved "the feel of a typescript folded into an envelope. And then the paycheck arriving in the mail" (240). Now, however, on reaching home, Alice finds her mother saying she will never recover from this tragic blow.

In her section, Fraidy immediately discounts Alice's theories. While acknowledging her love for her mother and her dutiful actions as a daughter during this crisis, Fraidy points out that Alice has not known her mother as long as Fraidy has, and, moreover, Alice emphasizes work too much: Beans once described Alice to Fraidy as "Her Holy Miss Righteousness" (242). Alice is a bit patronizing to her mother's old friends, says Fraidy, as when she expressed surprise that Fraidy had read Betty Friedan's *The Feminine Mystique*. When Alice says that women cannot be separated from their work, Fraidy disagrees: From her perspective, work is exhausting and demeaning. For Daisy, she believes, work was just the mechanism that released her sexual yearnings. Yet in the same breath she demeans "Daze" and her possible fling with Jay Dudley—Fraidy, after all, has kept a diary in which she records all fifty-three (possibly fifty-four) lovers she has had. "What do women want, Freud asked. The old fool, the charlatan. He knew what women wanted. They wanted nothing. Nothing was good enough. Everyone knew that. Everyone but me" (246). Although Fraidy loves Daisy, she really did travel to Ottawa because she thought that Daisy and she would "decode themselves" (247). She fails to get a rise out of Daisy, however, who once again lies flat on her back in her darkened room. And when she mails back the diary that Fraidy has unwittingly dropped on the carpet, Daisy's voice is mute. She merely addresses the envelope.

Cousin Beverly, reviewing the courage and spunk she used to have before she married, divorced, and gave birth to her baby, believes that Aunt Daisy is depressed about her children: she used to worry about Alice who had a very overbearing manner; Warren, who used to have acne but now, like Alice, has improved, attending the Eastman School of Music; and Joan, who now is the one to worry about, selling jewelry in New Mexico and living as a hippie. After examining the litany of Daisy's children, however, Beverly enunciates her real theory: "A person can make herself sick and that same person has to will herself to get well again, that's my personal theory" (250). Cousin Beverly knows Daisy unusually well.

After discovering a stack of essays that his mother had written in college, particularly the impressive one on a nineteenth-century Italian hero, Warren is overwhelmed at the difference between the mother he knew growing up, who rarely read a book and never talked about her education, and the young woman who wrote this essay: "Where did it go, my mother's intellectual ease and energy?" asks her only son (251). If he himself feels cheated, he concludes, then his mother must feel cheated as well. Someone, somewhere, he thinks, ruined her ability to think and to speak and thus "she must be in mourning for the squandering of herself" (252).

After coming home and hearing her mother replay the scene in which Pinky said he hoped his usurpation of her job wouldn't affect their friendship, Joan sees her mother "relishing" the marvelous drama of it all. Joan thinks that since this is the peak of her mother's emotional life, she should be left to enjoy "the salt of perfect pain" (253).

From Jay Dudley's perspective, Daisy wanted "a more permanent arrangement" even though she never said so. He protests that he was "very, very fond of her" but, after all, one marriage was "enough" for him, and so "it seemed best to put a little distance between us" (254). Completely self-centered and unable to fathom Daisy's relationship to her writing, he invents for her a broken heart brought on by their affair. More reprehensible than most readers had first thought, Jay Dudley actually fired Daisy rather than continue a relationship that made him nervous.

The next section elucidates the theory of Labina Anthony Greene Dukes. Despite her remarriage, Beans remains fixated on her first husband's rejection of her, speaking of herself as fragile and breakable. Implying rather than actually stating her theory, Beans thinks that Daisy has been worn down by innumerable disappointments.

Although a minor character whose voice we hear only once, Cora-Mae Milltown has a perspective that provides her with lucid insights into Daisy's depression. Cora-Mae sums up Daisy's situation succinctly: "First her mamma died, you see, then an old auntie who took care of her up in Canada, and now she's got no one in the world, only me" (255). Although Daisy left Indiana over two decades earlier, Cora-Mae knows whereof she speaks: she has not heard from her daughter in California for six or seven years. But the story is one with which she is familiar: "You can't make it go away. Your mama's inside you. You can feel her moving and breathing and sometimes you can hear her talking to you. . . ." and since Daisy never had a mother to worry about her and protect her, "How's she going to find her way? How's she going to be happy in her life?" (257).

Using the perspective of "the old Jew," Abram Skutari, who witnessed Mercy's death and Daisy's birth, Abram's grandson Scoot recounts his grandfather's history and his rise from peddler to founder and owner of a nationwide chain of retail outlets—and relates Abram's success to the courage he found in a long-ago "incident that changed his life" (259). His gaze was the last that Mercy saw, and he blessed the infant as he put an Albanian coin on her forehead. Unfortunately, however, "he felt as though he were blessing a stone, that nothing good could come out of his mouth" (260). Even as he gained strength from mingling his tears with those of Dr. Spears and signing both the birth and death certificates, "he grieved about that baby all his days, the curse that hung over it, its terrible anguish" (261). This stranger and his grandson, neither of whom knows Daisy, nonetheless understand the curse of emptiness and loneliness that she has inherited.

Daisy begins her own section, "Mrs. Flett's Theory," with the tongue-in-cheek statement that "[s]urely no one would expect Mrs. Flett to come up with a theory about her own suffering," since she's obviously incapable, "a mess, a nut case" (261). And indeed her soul has been "thrashing," reliving old hurts, "especially the old unmediated terror of abandonment" (262). But despite her terrible state, Daisy knows with certainty that she will eventually recover. She recalls reciting with Fraidy the old William Blake line, "Weep, weep, in notes of woe" and falling into each other with peals of laughter. She can endure only so much suffering: "That's Daisy for you"—and with the resurrection of her first name, she convinces us that recovery is imminent: "all this suffering will be washed away. Any day now" (262).

EASE, 1977

This chapter opens on the eve of Daisy's trip to the Orkney Islands. Completely recovered from her depression twelve years earlier (she has learned to keep her hands busy), Daisy plans to accompany her great-niece Victoria on this excursion, a research trip for Victoria who is now a paleo-botanist like her great-uncle Barker, and, like her mother Beverly, who died four years earlier, is completely devoted to Aunt Daisy. The love they share is genuine, and Victoria sincerely tries to help Aunt Daisy without being condescending or patronizing (she believes, for instance, that a favor the young can do for the old is to argue with them and rouse them to debate). Daisy has been interested in researching her family tree for a long time, but focuses on her father, Cuyler Goodwill and her father-in-law, Magnus Flett. Privately, Victoria believes that Daisy is transferring her search for information about her mother to these two male figures, that they constitute a red herring of sorts, and she may very well be correct. Victoria has no desire to know more about her own father—"in fact, she doesn't give one golden fuck" (269). Still, she does not know her aunt as well as she thinks she does. For example, Daisy has read a good many more books—memoirs, autobiographies, social histories—than Victoria suspects.

Daisy lives in Bayside Towers, a three-bedroom condo in a Sarasota development near both Fraidy Hoyt and Beans Green Dukes Kavanaugh, whose third marriage is to Bud Kavanaugh. She still gardens, now focusing on the tropical plants that crowd her Sarasota balcony. Daisy treats us to a lingering insight into Cuyler as, dying from a stroke in the backyard of his cottage on Lemon Lake, his mind tries doggedly to recall the name of his first wife Mercy. It is his favorite season, April, with the forsythia, lilac and mock orange bushes obscuring his body from the view of passersby. He decides to stop building his pyramid, but tries to recall what he put in the metal box at its base—and finally, he recalls both the fact of the wedding ring and the name of his wife Mercy. He "may or may not" have thought about his only daughter in these final moments of his life. Although he died in 1955, his daughter's feats of imagination can replay his death in any way she likes, even now, "in the sun-blessed state of Florida." Switching momentarily to the first person, the narrator states that although Mrs. Flett recovered from her "nervous torment" of twelve years ago, "a kind of rancor underlies her existence still: the recognition that she belongs to no one" (281). Perhaps, suggests the narrator, that is why she continues to think about the two fathers, "hurling herself at the emptiness she was handed at birth" (281).

At this point we learn that despite the cheerful facade she manages to maintain, she does have her moments where she lies on her bed with tears in her eyes, understanding that she has learned to accept "doses of disabling information" and then stir "them with the spoon of her longing" (282). Once again, her imagination—that indispensable tool of a writer, particularly a memoirist or biographer—holds her steady: "She enlarges on the available material, extends, shrinks, reshapes what's offered; this mixed potion is her life" (282). Occasionally she makes a major subtraction, as when Fraidy Hoyt almost definitely sees Maria Goodwill walking down the street on an elderly gentleman's arm: this scenario simply will not do, since Daisy has already written Maria back into "her Italian village and transformed her into a black draped figure of mourning with a bowl of knitting in her lap" (283).

The scene then switches to a hilarious hodgepodge of advice to Daisy, who has not traveled to Europe since 1927. She is told to take everything from umbrellas to ponchos to walking shoes to Perma-press blouses, depending on whether the adviser is one of her children, Victoria, Fraidy or Beans. And after a somewhat tense beginning at the airport, when Victoria surprises Daisy by introducing Lewis Roy, her instructor, who will be accompanying them to the Orkneys, they reach the cemetery at Stromness and find that the name Flett stretches back several centuries.

Daisy has taken this trip as part of her quest for Magnus Flett who, in different circumstances, "might have had things to say" to her and she to him (291). Mr. Sinclair, the proprietor of their hotel, informs them that Magnus is alive and well at 115, living next door and famous throughout the Orkneys for having memorized the entire novel of *Jane Eyre*. Daisy inexplicably postpones her visit to him, pre-ferring instead to explore the Orkneys with Mr. Sinclair, and to dis-cover that "the Orkney greenness is deceptive. What looks like yards of fertile black earth is only a thin covering over beds of layered rock," and she understands why so many stonecutters originated in the Orkney Islands. Magnus himself worked in the quarries until he was sixty-five. Still, Daisy postpones seeing Magnus so that she can visit "the hugeness" of the rocks, the sea below, the spreading moorland, and she suddenly realizes that she feels great happiness. She experi-ences a feeling similar to the goal of Victoria and Roy: they are look-ing for tracings of "buried life," life turned to stone, "a small rock chip imprinted with the outline of a leaf. Or a primitive flower" (301).

When at last Daisy encounters Magnus Flett, she carries her romanticized view of him—"Magnus, the wanderer, the suffering

modern man"—an outsider as she herself has been an outsider, an
orphan seeking refuge (305). Indeed, given his incontinence, his
inability to communicate with her or recognize the names of his
wife Clarentine and son Barker, one would expect her to be disap-
pointed. And yes, in time she will need to revise the experience in
her artist-survivor's way—but the immediate effect of her visit is one
that leaves her feeling buoyant and unburdened: "Oh. She is young
and strong again. Look at the way she walks freely out the door and
down the narrow stone street of Stromness, tossing her hair in the
fine light" (307). Carol Shields herself has recently experienced a
similar phenomenon: "Just today [in March 2001] I noticed that, in
the presence of extreme old age, I was so young compared to everyone there. These people were all bedridden. I left with a kind of
relief, just as Daisy did, from that romanticism that binds you—it
gives you some buoyancy."

ILLNESS AND DECLINE, 1985

As the chapter title implies, Daisy enters the difficult years of sick-
ness and old age. If there is poetic justice—and Shields ensures that
there is—Daisy's decline is initiated while engaged in an activity
that she loves: as she waters some geraniums on the south side of
her balcony, she has a heart attack that causes her to fall and break
both knees.

Now at age eighty she is hospitalized at the Sarasota Memorial
Hospital and her body lets her down: she has a double bypass and a
cancerous kidney that is immediately removed. As she experiences
drug-induced dreams and nightmares, her imaginative process continues; she can still march "straight into the machinery of invention.
. . . Sketching vivid scenery. Laying out conversations, arguments"
(311). Yet she is filled with "pain and bewilderment" (314), and her
children learn that she will never walk again. She is cheered,

however, by the faithful visits of the Flowers—Lily, Myrtle, and Glad who, together with Daisy, make up the bridge foursome so terribly important to Daisy after she lost Fraidy to senility and Beans to a sudden death in the late 1970s. A woman named Iris waits to join the foursome whenever the next opening should occur.

Shields notes that "Daisy has had good luck in her life in that she was blessed with good women friends, and was lucky to have had these friends from childhood. Later, after she lost them, she had the Flowers in Sarasota. Creating this group was something I just grew into . . . my own parents live in Florida, and bridge is very important to my father . . . he has a group he plays with." All four of the Flowers are well-off widows who love to laugh; they especially like to joke about dying: When other residents of Bayside Towers ask how the Flowers are blooming, one will respond, "Fading fast," and another, "but holding firm!" or "Here's to another year and let's hope it's above ground!" (319). Again, Shields draws on her own experience here, recalling that she first noticed humor among the aging in her own family. Says Shields, "I had all these old aunts who, even though they might be deaf or blind, would say, 'I hope we're all alive next year,' and then go into peals of laughter."

Daisy has never been religious—she has been too busy during her lifetime, preoccupied with her husband, her family, her many tasks—but now, lying in the hospital, she relishes a secret happiness: Her hospital bracelet mistakenly omits the name "Flett" and instead reads "Daisy Goodwill," her original girlhood name before she became Mrs. Flett or Grandma Flett, and Daisy cherishes this secret as "the outward sign of her soul" (320). When the young Reverend Rick makes his visits after her surgery, she does not tell him that this name on this bracelet is her soul, not the one Reverend Rick tries to have her embrace. And in addition to the bracelet is her forgotten knowledge of "the small primal piece of herself that came unshaped into the world," prompting her realization that "I'm still in here," despite the hospital, the losses, the loneliness she has endured (322). She builds relationships with Jubilee and the other hospital staffers, but doing so—living up to their images of her as "an old sweetie-pie, a fighter, a real-lady, a non-complainer"—frequently subsumes the Daisy Goodwill who has recently surfaced.

The move to the Canary Palms Convalescent Home—too far from the Flowers, too far from Jubilee—might have finished off a weaker woman, but ultimately Daisy demonstrates the innate optimism that saves her time after time. Initially, though, when Alice visits each day, both mother and daughter have difficulty adapting to the new situation: "I'm not myself," complains Daisy, and when she says she cannot hear Alice's response because of the screams of another patient, Alice repeats, "I'm not myself either" (324-325). Much as Daisy had invented thrilling dialogues for her reunion with Barker on her trip to Ottawa from Indiana, Alice now tries to invent meaningful mother-daughter dialogue, but instead their conversation epitomizes the mundane as they discuss hospital food, other patients, doctor visits. Bleakly, Alice realizes that her mother's world has shrunk to such an extent that all her possessions fit into one drawer.

On her good days, though, Daisy "is still in there." Then she reads the newspapers, cover-to-cover, and one day reads the remarkable fact that eleven North Americans each year are killed by vending machines. By the time she relates this fact to Alice, she reports that Pinky Fulham was the victim of a soft drinks vending machine, and when Alice asks how she heard this news, Daisy innocently replies that she read about it recently. Carol Shields, when asked if Daisy imagined this bizarre death, replied, "Yes, she made up his death!" adding, "The vending machine that 'kills' Pinky Fulham I found among some odd and little known facts in *The Globe and Mail*." Indeed, Daisy is surprised that humor extends into old age, as does vanity. In a lengthy flashback, Daisy recalls her girlhood in Clarentine Flett's garden, conjuring up the rich and varied sensations of pancakes, a rainbow, snow, summer grass—and learning the meaning of "daisy": Day's Eye. The sad irony, of course, is the pun on the word "Eye": Daisy has so little self that she rarely uses the word "I." We all, says the third-person narrator, require "at least one witness, but Mrs. Flett has not had this privilege. This is what breaks her heart. What she can't bear. Even now, eighty years old" (339). Daisy knows she must conclude with imagination . . . and she asks, "What is the story of a life? A chronicle of fact or a skillfully wrought impression?" (340) She needs someone to listen to her.

DEATH

Daisy lives for a number of years into the 1990s. The most important technique to note in this final chapter, as Shields herself emphasizes, is that "she's still alive, thinking of the meatloaf, the hat, and so forth. She's imagining what's happening." The random lists—of Daisy's bridal lingerie, embroidery, first marriage papers, garden club luncheon plans, a recipe for lemon pudding, a shopping list, a list of books from *Black Beauty* to *Murder in the Meantime*, a must-do list, even her medical problems—are pieces of paper that she imagines her family finding and speculating about. Quite early in the chapter, she ponders the fact that, "though she knew she had been loved in her life," she had never heard "I love you, Daisy" (345). And in the midst of all these lists, she intones—or cries out—"I'm still here, oh, oh" (352). Listening to the comments that she imagines at her death, we know that some are correct (that she lived in the wrong age [352]) and others incorrect (that she never slept with Jay Dudley [354]).

Near the very end she finally sees herself as stone, merging with the body of her dead mother, a goal it has taken her an entire lifetime to reach—but is it too little, too late? Shields emphasizes that she knew that as Daisy grew older and more infirm, "I was working toward one sentence: 'I am not at peace.' I knew I was working toward that, and I didn't want to write it because I like to think people are at peace." Daisy lived a long life and survived numerous blows and disappointments—but the despairing thought is that she never did come to terms with her own self. The best she could do was to continue her "blend of distortion and omission," and her understanding that "there are millions, billions, of other men and women in the world who wake up early in their separate beds, greedy for the substance of their own lives, but obliged every day to reinvent themselves" (283). At the very end, however, she sees "nothing, nothing, that is, but the deep, shared common distress of men and women, and how little they are allowed, finally, to say" (359). In every sense of the word, this seemingly unremarkable woman is in fact remarkable. The stories of her life not only continue to reverberate in our consciousness, but force each of us to question our revisions, additions and subtractions, and our own blends of fact and fantasy.

3

The Novel's Reception

*T*he Stone Diaries won the Governor General's Award in Canada in 1993, the Pulitzer Prize for Fiction in 1995, and the National Book Critics Circle Award in 1995. It was also short-listed for England's Booker Prize in 1994, and won an ABBY (American Bookseller Book of the Year) award in 1995. The Canadian Bookseller's Association named Carol Shields Author of the Year in 1997. Mindy Warner, senior editor at Viking Penguin, her U. S. publisher, says "it couldn't have happened to a better writer or a nicer person. I adore her."

The book has received rave reviews from nearly every critic. Atypical and clearly in the minority are two less-than-stellar analyses of the novel by Andy Solomon and Geraldine Sherman. Solomon states that The Stone Diaries is not Shields's best novel: "In the attempt to tell the stories of too many uneventful lives from too many points of view, much of Shields's native irony, twisty plots, and light hearted sarcasm disappear. Perhaps the historical or genealogical epic is not her genre" (Solomon 2).   In a similar manner, Geraldine Sherman suggests that, "in the end, Daisy Goodwill's tiny secrets and personal disappointments cannot bear the strain of the novel's high ambitions and overbearing technique" (Sherman 170). Other than these two, however, the critics generally find the novel brilliantly innovative and successful in achieving sympathy for the unlikely hero and her equally unlikely friends and family. Samplings from the critics of Canada, the United States (both of which gave her their highest awards), and England (which shortlisted her for theirs) suggest a near-unanimous approval of the award-winning work. Although various reviewers focus on different strengths of the novel, they all seem in accord with the words of the New York Times reviewer who astutely observes that "*The Stone Diaries* reminds us again why literature matters."

Although, in the main, most of the Canadian and British reviews appeared shortly after publication of *The Stone Diaries* in 1993 while the American commentary appeared in 1995 (the United States was slow to respond until after the novel was awarded the Pulitzer Prize), critics have universally praised Shields's style, finding it, in Clara Thomas's words, "delicate, intricate, witty, ironic, [and] humorous." Most of the reviews focus on one or more of the following categories: Shields's use of lyrical language, including her employment of metaphor, her attention to detail, and her sense of humor; her wisdom, including her insights into the meaning of even the seemingly irrelevant aspects of a life; her sympathetic treatment of her characters and her clear testament to the significance of "unremarkable" people, particularly her protagonist; and her deliberate blurring of the fine line between biography or autobiography and fiction.

"Lyrically written and always entertaining, *The Stone Diaries* is Shields' most accomplished novel to date," says Diane Turbide, and she is echoed in a *Books in Canada* review that finds the novel "richly detailed, engrossing [and] unsentimental," while *Publisher's Weekly* praises the "elegant imagery" that characterizes the novel. Occasionally, reviewers seem so genuinely moved by Shields's language that they respond in a similar vein, as in the remarkable imagery found in Jay Parini's review: "Her words ring like stones in a brook, chilled and perfected; the syntax rushes like water, tumbling with the slight forward tilt that makes for narrative. The reader is caught in whirlpools and eddies, swirled, then launched farther downstream" (Parini 173).

Nor does any critic seem to fall into the trap of mistaking eloquence for thinness or insubstantiality. *The Times Literary Supplement* reviewer comments on the intelligence and irreverence that mingle with the lyricism: "It is characteristic of Carol Shields to deal equally in astringency and good humour. Her novels . . . are buoyant and lucid; they are also skeptical, argumentative and surprising," and Kathryn Hughes notes the "miraculous meeting of intellectual rigour and imaginative flow" (Hughes 40). Praised by a *Kirkus* reviewer for her "ironic wisdom" that "dazzle[s]" its readers, and by a *Books in Canada* critic for her "engrossing, unsentimental" wisdom, another reviewer, Merna Summers, singles out Shields for producing a book containing not a single page "that does not delight, does not contain something quotable. " A *People Weekly* reviewer calls the novel an "absorbing, subtly comic, beautifully crafted narrative that teaches, entertains and moves to tears."

Shields's attention to the "small things that matter," as the *Mirabella* reviewer puts it, is highly relevant to an appreciation of *The Stone Diaries*, and few readers fail to comment on this point. In Canada at this time, "there is no one writing," declares Clara Thomas, "who has such a noticing eye and a joyous talent for the recording of the myriad details of a dailiness as Carol Shields" (Clara Thomas 160), and the *Kirkus* reviewer notes the high quality of Shields's achievements "with this latest exploration of domestic plenitude and paucity" or, in the words of the *Reading* critic, this "wise and unusual novel that makes the ordinary extra-ordinary." Moreover, while a number of reviewers have praised Shields for creating in Daisy an ordinary protagonist, an "Everywoman," not everyone would agree: "No one," declares the *McGill* reviewer, "in a Shields novel is ordinary," and certainly there has been no shortage of praise for Shields's ability to create "compelling characters" (*McGill* 175; *Publisher's Weekly* December 13, 1993, v. 240, no. 50, p. 60 (2). The *Gentleman's Quarterly* critic notes Shields's "poetic and audacious" sensitivity to the "inner lives of the inarticulate."

In this "strange and beautiful novel" numerous critics, including both Rhoda Koenig and Hughes emphasize the way Shields infuses the ordinary with a sense of both pleasure and mystery (Koenig 172; Hughes 40). *The Stone Diaries* is "a serious exploration of the essential mystery of human lives," asserts *Publisher's Weekly*, particularly, adds the *Reading* reviewer, the "mysteries of love, culture and spirituality shimmering beneath the surface of a quiet woman's life." Indeed, principally because the novel and its narrator recognize this essential mystery, Shields—even if we were not living in a postmodern era—would appear justified in trying startling new ways to examine and interpret an individual life. *The Stone Diaries* is Shields's "playful send-up of the art of biography," says the *Publisher's Weekly* reviewer, and in so doing she demonstrates to us that no biography can lay claim to the "only" version of the truth. Thus the novel not only looks at the myriad ways of telling the story of a life, but it also engages in a "sharp-as-tacks" exploration of the limitations of the traditional autobiography.

When short-listing Shields for the Booker Prize, the judges praised her for "giving us a new kind of heroine" (qtd. Summers 171), and surely Daisy is unlike any other modern woman protagonist: Laura Van Tuyl Clayton agrees, noting that "For those of us fatigued by all this fictional heroism, author Carol Shields has torpedoed the notion that only nervous excitement and derring-do can generate a gripping story" (Clayton 174). Shields's portrait of Daisy, in fact, is so singular and original that some reviewers are at a loss as to whether it is a novel for a general audience or one for women only. While Shields herself believes that the lives of men and women are equally viable, equally worthy, Gail Pool insists that "It is very much a woman's story" (Pool 3), and writer-critic Anita Brookner declares that the appeal of The Stone Diaries lies "principally" with "women readers," but that this appeal is "of an altogether superior kind" (Brookner 289). In a similar vein, noting the allusions to major twentieth-century events during Daisy's lifetime, the Cosmopolitan reviewer praises Shields for the way she subtly employs "Daisy's life and death to explore the history of women in the twentieth century."

Another sign of the increasing awareness that The Stone Diaries is a notable novel with genuine staying power is in the growing number of scholarly articles devoted to close scrutiny and analysis of the myriad facets of this novel, which continues to provide a rich and seemingly endless source of speculation and satisfaction. Simone Vauthier, for instance, finds The Stone Diaries intriguing from the perspective of chaos theory. While Vauthier claims no specific knowledge of scientific and philosophical assumptions for either herself or the author, Shields has in fact publicly mentioned chaos theory as a fascinating field with various possibilities for explaining random human behavior ("Life and Times"). Vauthier's premise — that versions of chaos theory, however general and even distorted, have entered our late twentieth-century consciousness so that even the most "unscientifically minded" of us are "dimly aware" of the theory. By so framing her rationale, Vauthier sounds much like Shields when Shields describes the way she may be unconsciously influenced by other writers: "I think it's in the drinking water, don't you?" In her article, Vauthier builds a compelling case based on the novel's blending of order and disorder, from the uncertainty of the fictional mode (autobiography? biography? fiction?) to the uncertainty of Daisy's character, to the deliberate interruptions of chapter chronology and the role of chance, accident, and coincidence in the lives presented in the novel.[21]

Winifred Mellor bases her essay on the idea that when one reveals personal details about oneself, one is in fact engaging in a creation of self. Her theory has an even more specific basis in Shields herself, who is on record as saying that the individual is capable of change, of willing herself or himself into a different persona. Mellor proceeds to examine Daisy's split self and Shields's initially confusing but nearly mesmerizing depiction of that self through the changing narrative perspectives of first and third person, culminating in the brilliantly provocative sentence where, after weeks in the sick room, Daisy's use of "me" and "her" conflates: "The long days of isolation, of silence, the torment of boredom—all these passed down on me, on young Daisy Goodwin and emptied her out" (75). Mellor's analysis helps illuminate the difficulties of self-revelation, self-creation, and life-writing, particularly if the self is a woman.

Gordon E. Slethaug, too, examines *The Stone Diaries* and chaos theory, with specific attention to Carol Shields's use of the metaphor of stones that culminates in Daisy's merging with her mother. Clara Thomas compares *The Republic of Love* and *The Stone Diaries* in terms of Shields's evolving use of chance and the deceptiveness of appearances. Thomas, unlike the author herself, does not find *The Stone Diaries* despairing: ""Some readers call it 'sad,' but to me, if it is sad it is in the way that Wordsworth's 'Tintern Abbey' is sad, an affirmation of life that far outweighs the melancholy of its 'still, sad music of humanity'" (Thomas 157). Thomas, too, alludes to Carol Shields's belief in the ability to change and transcend, and, although she can understand why some younger women feel dismayed at Daisy's seeming melancholy and wasted years, sees Daisy optimistically.

The scholarship on *The Stone Diaries* will expand rather than diminish. Other possible areas for study, both within *The Stone*

Diaries and in comparison with other fictional and autobiographical works include the following: more analyses of the mother-daughter relationship; the psychology of orphanhood; Daisy's "sadness" versus her strength of imagination; the use of the unreliable narrator; the nature of fiction and memoir, specifically the influential role of others in defining the individual; and the striking similarities between Carol Shields and Edith Wharton.

Whatever the individual consensus, in writing *The Stone Diaries* Carol Shields took "unusual risks" in producing "a work of great but unconventional ambition" (Messud 171). The "seamlessly developed" narrative has resulted in "an impeccable performance."

4

The Novel's Performance

*T*he Stone Diaries has performed and sold exceptionally well. At this writing, sales figures, available through March, 2000, provide useful testaments to the novel's popularity and staying power: in Canada, *The Stone Diaries* has sold 289,000 copies, in the United Kingdom, 226,000, and in the United States, 675,000. The novel continues to sell well. In May, 2001, it was the best-selling novel of all Shields's works offered on the Barnes and Noble website, and on amazon.com was, among her works, selling second only to her recently published *Jane Austen*. In addition to healthy and continuous reprints in these three countries, it has been translated and published in Sweden, Norway, Italy, and the Netherlands (1994); Germany and Denmark (1995); Spain (1996, 1997), Greece, Korea, Taiwan, Brazil, and Japan (1996); Israel, the Czech Republic, Turkey, and Iceland (1997); Poland, Portugal, Estonia, Hungary, and Croatia (1997–98); France, Sweden, Norway, Denmark, the Netherlands, Germany, Finland, Greece, and Catalania (1998); Israel, China, Poland, Spain, and Brazil (1999); and Finland (2000). As the list shows, the novel has been reprinted three times in Spain, where it is exceedingly popular, twice in Brazil, twice in Sweden, twice in Finland, twice in the Netherlands, and twice in Norway, Greece, Israel, and Poland.

Shields's work is receiving an unprecedented amount of attention for a so-called "literary" writer. A feature-length film of *The Stone Diaries* is in the planning stages with Toronto's Rhombus Media, the company responsible for *32 Short Films about Glenn Gould* and *The Red Violin*. Cynthia Scott, who directed *In the Company of Strangers*, is slated to direct the film, whose screenplay is being written by Semi Chellas, author of screenplays for *A Life Before This* and *Dead Aviators*. In April, 2001, a musical version of Shields's novel, *Larry's Party*, written by Richard Ouzounian and Marek Norman, was performed at the Manitoba Theatre Centre; and in July, 2001, the film version of her novel, *The Republic of Love*, is scheduled to begin shooting in Winnipeg. It will be directed by Deepa Mehta, who also wrote the screenplay. Shields's 1987 novel, *Swann: A Mystery*, was adapted by Toronto based screenwriter David Young in a Canadian-British co-production of a feature-length film. Composer Paul MacIntyre has written the opera score for Shields's play, *Thirteen Hands*. The play itself has been performed at several major Canadian theaters.

The popularity of Shields's work extends beyond the visual media to that of radio. In an article in the *Edmonton Journal*, Gordon Morash details the increased "global literary exploration" fostered by the 1997 partnership between Goose Lane, one of Canada's fine small presses, and the CBC: together they packaged the radio network's short story series, *Between the Covers*, both on audiotape and CD, and as an anthology entitled *Emergent Voices* (1997). With 24 short story titles, the anthology actually demonstrates the history of the short story in Canada, with writers ranging from such "international players" as Carol Shields and Michael Ondaatje, to the younger Canadians, Janette Turner Hospital, and Audrey Thomas, among others. As is to be expected, Shields's short stories are represented in numerous anthologies such as that edited by Birk Sproxton, *Great Stories from the Prairies*, scheduled for publication in 2001.

The increasing significance of *The Stone Diaries* may also be measured by the notable—and extremely varied—literary company in which Shields is regularly included both in and out of the academy. Although many universities do not yet list their courses online, a search of the Internet shows classroom use of *The Stone Diaries* for two very different sorts of literature courses. At the University of Vermont, *The Stone Diaries* is being taught in the winter term, 2001, in a class called "The Contemporary American Novel." Other novels to be studied with *The Stone Diaries* include Ralph Ellison's *Invisible Man*, Toni Morrison's *The Bluest Eye*, Vladimir Nabokov's *Lolita*, Louise Erdrich's *Tracks*, Art Speigelman's *Maus I and II*, and Sherman Alexie's *Reservation Blues*. In a different vein altogether, Shields' experimentation with the biographical and autobiographical form is reflected in the current vogue in memoir and autobiography, from Frank McCourt's best-selling *Angela's Ashes* to "Biography," the popular Arts & Entertainment TV series. At the University of Pennsylvania, in a course called "Women and Literature: The Autobiographical Form," *The Stone Diaries* is being studied alongside memoirs and autobiographies by such writers as Isak Dinesen, Marguerite Duras, bell hooks, Maxine Hong Kingston, and Doris Lessing. A comparison of these two groups of extremely varied writers testify still further to Carol Shields's own versatility, to the different ways she may be read and interpreted, and even to the different geographical contexts in which she may be studied.

In addition, Wilder Penfield points out that, as a Pulitzer Prize winner, Shields is in the company of other distinguished Pulitzer Prize recipients who wrote such twentieth century classics as *The Good Earth* (Pearl Buck), *Gone With the Wind* (Margaret Mitchell),

The Yearling (Marjorie Kinnan Rawlings), *The Grapes of Wrath* (Steinbeck), *The Caine Mutiny* (Herman Wouk), *The Old Man and the Sea* (Ernest Hemingway), *A Death in the Family* (James Agee and Walker Evans), and *To Kill a Mockingbird* (Harper Lee). Shields is the increasing subject of scholarly and academic research. At the last count before this book went to press, the Modern Language Association, the premier bibliography for academic articles and books, listed twenty-eight articles devoted to interpretation of Shields's many books, with the bulk of them looking at *The Stone Diaries* and *Swann*. Overall, in terms of reviews, journal articles, book chapters, and interviews, over 130 were devoted to Carol Shields. Although there is as yet no Carol Shields website *per se*, an increasing number of links appear on the Internet. Penguin Putnam offers a lengthy list of discussion questions for readers (available on the Penguin Putnam website, as well as amazon.com and barnesandnoble.com websites) along with an interview with the author.[22]

5

Further Reading and Discussion Questions

The Stone Diaries engages and challenges readers in many ways, posing implicit questions that are key to interpreting and understanding the novel. The text itself is the most important source, of course, giving rise to numerous questions that thoughtful readers can ask themselves, or discuss with other readers in a book discussion group. In addition to the thought-provoking issues and ideas that emerge from the text of *The Stone Diaries*, the last few years have produced a plethora of secondary material in the form of reviews, journal articles, interviews, and book chapters devoted to Carol Shields and *The Stone Diaries*. Many of these are available in libraries, and an increasing number are available online. In any case, this book contains some of the most significant observations by critics of Carol Shields' work, and these should be useful to the reader seeking additional information. Questions may also be divided into narrower, more specific ones that help pinpoint a character or an idea; while the broader, more general ones seek to contextualize the novel as a whole. There are questions arising from Carol Shields's biography, too, as detailed in interviews and, especially, in the CBC "Life and Times" documentary that takes her up to March, 2001.

SPECIFIC QUESTIONS ABOUT THE TEXT OF *THE STONE DIARIES*

1. The narrator calls Mercy a "flour barrel baby," a phenomenon unknown in Canada but, according to Shields, "there really were flour barrel babies in Burgundy, France." Do you view the birth scene as Mercy speaking, in part, through Daisy? or do you see the scene as Daisy's total invention of a mother she never knew? Do you think Daisy's life would have turned out better or worse if her mother had not died?

2. If Daisy misses her mother to the degree that most readers believe, why does she travel so far to seek out Magnus Flett, her father-in-law, whom she never even met?

3. How do you characterize the relationship between Clarentine Flett and Mercy Goodwill?

4. How important are Daisy's early years with Aunt Clarentine and her son Barker? Do you see her developing in any sort of positive way, or, to the contrary, do you believe she is damaged?

5. Strictly speaking, says Shields, "there was no Goodwill Tower, but I'm very interested in what the French call 'brute art,' created by insane people and prisoners—tomato soup towers, for instance—for no reason we can fathom, with no connection or relation to art as we know it." Do you view Cuyler Goodwill's creation an obsession? a work of art? a combination of both?

6. What do you make of the young Barker Flett and his obsession with the western lady's slipper that sublimates "his most primitive urges" (Parini 173)?

7. Both Cuyler Goodwill and Magnus Flett lose their wives at about the time that Daisy is born. Cuyler builds a monument to Mercy and Magnus starts to read novels. Are the two men more alike than different?

8. Shields does not use much detail to describe Daisy's train trip with her father from Winnipeg to Bloomington, Indiana, yet she

suggests it was significant. How does Shields characterize Daisy's feelings about this reunion with her father eleven years after her birth?

9. According to Fitzgerald, the switch from first person in 1905 to third in 1916 marks Daisy's failure to establish her own identity or even a language that would help make that discovery possible (Fitzgerald 169). Other critics view it as a challenge she can meet and overcome. Which view seems more accurate?

10. Shields comments that "Daisy has had good luck in her life in that she was blessed with good women friends, and was lucky to have had these friends from childhood. Later, after she lost them, she had the Flowers in Sarasota." How do you characterize Beans and Fraidy? Can you differentiate between them? Do they remain of equal importance to Daisy?

11. Speaking of the Flowers, Shields says that "creating this group was something I just grew into . . . my own parents live in Florida, and bridge is very important to my father . . . he has a group he plays with." What do you think, specifically, about the role of the Flowers?

12. In portraying Daisy, Shields reveals that she "tried in each chapter to have a moment of clarity for Daisy, usually when she was lying on her back (although in one chapter she's sitting on the train)." Do these moments help elucidate Daisy's character?

13. Shields realizes that "there is humor among the aging, too, as when Daisy and the other Flowers make jokes about dying. I had all these old aunts who, even though they might be deaf or blind, would say, 'I hope we're all alive next year,' and then go into peals of laughter." Does her use of humor help mitigate the sadness in Daisy's life?

14. Do you believe that Daisy's first husband, Harold Hoad, committed suicide? If not, what do you think caused his fall from the window ledge?

15. How important a role does Mrs. Arthur Hoad play in Daisy's life?

16. After her father marries Maria, Daisy plans her own trip from Indiana to Canada. Does this trip give us any new indication about her potential or her character?

17. Daisy seems to know that the trip will end with her marriage to Barker and her semi-permanent return to Canada. Do you think her second marriage is based on romantic love, or do you see more complicated reasons for her return to Barker?

18. Do you have any reasons for thinking that Daisy is a good mother?

19. Are you surprised that Daisy is such a success when she becomes Mrs. Green Thumb?

20. On the loss of her job, does Daisy's deep depression surprise you, or did you find indications that suggested it was coming?

21. After her move to Sarasota, to what degree do you think Daisy has come to terms with herself?

GENERAL QUESTIONS ARISING FROM THE TEXT

1. Shields knows, admires, and considered using W. H. Auden's poem, "In Praise of Limestone" as an epigraph for the novel. Would it have worked as well as the one she uses in the published novel?

2. What is your reaction to Shields's use of metaphor? Consider, for instance, the plentiful use of stones throughout the novel, and the significance of flowers, the wedding ring, and the references to Eden or paradise. Do these add to your enjoyment of the novel in a meaningful way?

3. Recall, too, Shields's comment that, "I had a working title of 'Stone and Flower,' but that was too heavily symbolic, and it led too easily to gender stereotypes. I also thought of 'Daisy Goodwill: A Life,' and 'Monument.'" Does the published title seem to fit the novel?

4. How effective do you find Shields's use of narrative point of view, especially when Daisy switches from first person to third, or from her own viewpoint to that of another character?

5. How does Shields present Daisy in terms of her attitude toward sex? Does Daisy seem typical of her era?

6. What role does imagination play in this novel? Is it possible to separate Daisy's own use of imagination from the close relationship between imagination and art? between art and the story of a life?

7. Would you say that Shields treats men and women with equal respect in *The Stone Diaries*?

8. In the end, do you find this book a despairing view of a woman's life, or do you believe that Daisy finds some measure of happiness?

9. Do you agree with one of Daisy's children's statements at the end, that Daisy was born in the wrong century?

10. As in many of her novels, Shields alludes to the fact that Americans know very little about Canada. "No one pays attention to Canada," she says matter of factly. "I grew up in Illinois, and don't think I could even spell Saskatchewan." With Magnus and Cuyler, however, "I did try to use historical accuracy in that many men from the Orkney Islands emigrated to Canada, and it's also true that when stonecutting fell on bad times, they went to Indiana." Do you see other instances of Canadian history illuminating the narrative?

11. Shields suggests that one of the reasons so many good writers come from Canada today is that "we're writing from the edge, from the edge of the continent, the forehead of North America," and that position is conducive to emerging voices and views. Further, Canada has produced no Faulkners or Hemingways "to intimidate our young male writers" (Hollenberg 9). Does this statement seem accurate to you?

INFLUENCES FROM OTHER WRITERS

Although Carol Shields has mentioned a few specific writers who have influenced her own work—writers from Jane Austen and Virginia Woolf to Gabriella Roy, Alice Munro, Mavis Gallant, and Philip Larkin—as a postmodernist writer, she has also recognized the unconscious and possibly serendipitous influences of others. She says, for instance, "I've read Toni Morrison and Edith Wharton—in fact, I reviewed *Paradise* for the *Washington Post*. But if there are influences from these writers—or from Henry James (Daisy Miller) or Scott Fitzgerald (Daisy Buchanan), it's at a subconscious level." She continues, saying that she has read Harriet Doeer, too, quite recently, in fact: "I have a 'bibliotherapist' friend who gave me Harriet Doerr's *Stones for Ibarra* to read . . . no, I didn't feel that she consciously influenced me, but I think these things are in the drinking water, don't you?" Like any writer whose work is richly conceived and richly drawn, Shields is reminiscent of other authors in various respects. As pointed out elsewhere, Shields, having won the Pulitzer Prize, finds herself in some very august company. Do you find echoes of other writers you've read, either earlier or contemporary ones?

1. Are there possible allusions in *Stone Diaries* to Mercy in Toni Morrison's *Song of Solomon*? To Daisy in Henry James's *Daisy Miller* and F. Scott Fitzgerald's Daisy Buchanan in *The Great Gatsby*?

2. The emphasis on the solidity and permanence of stones suggests Harriet Doerr's novel, *Stones for Ibarra*. Do you see other similarities between the two novels?

3. Edith Wharton famously talked about the information she omitted from her novels and stories, explaining her belief that no one can "reach truth" alone, and that there are many different versions of it. She believed that reading, as well as writing, "should be a creative act" and she counted on her readers to meet her "halfway"

to fill in "the gaps of my narrative." This technique sounds remarkably like the one Shields uses in *The Stone Diaries*. Do you see other resemblances between Wharton and Shields?

4. At several stages of this novel, Daisy might be compared to Addie Bundren of Faulkner's *As I Lay Dying*, from her vague dissatisfaction with her marriage, to the not-quite-distinguishable voices of her children at the end as Daisy lies dying, to her choice to be buried away from her husband. Do you find this a valid comparison?

5. Lisa Sims-Brandon has written an article demonstrating the ironic contrast between Kate Chopin's Edna Pontellier of *The Awakening*, who experiences a memorable "awakening," to Daisy Flett, who appears to be "sleepwalking." Do you see any convergence between the two heroines?

6. In Shields's use of newspaper clippings, lists, and the like, her tone is reminiscent of that of the newspaper articles in Fannie Flagg's *Fried Green Tomatoes at the Whistle Stop Cafe*. Regardless of whether you see any similarities between the two novels, do you find the newspaper motif an effective way of demonstrating the "way it was" during a particular era?

7. Barbara Kingsolver's novel, *Prodigal Summer*, is striking in the way she uses the lady's-slipper as a highly erotic metaphor. What other similarities do you see between *Prodigal Summer* and *The Stone Diaries*?

8. Read such Canadian writers as Alice Munro, Margaret Atwood, and Mavis Gallant, and compare their themes and techniques with those of Carol Shields. Several books and essay collections (*Private and Fictional Worlds: Canadian Women Novelists of the 1970s and 1980s*, by Coral Ann Howells; *The Canadian Post-Modern*, by Linda Hutcheon; *Sub/Version: Canadian Fiction by Women*, by Lorna Irvine; and *Canadian Women Writing Fiction*, edited by Mickey Pearlman) help provide background material.

SUGGESTED READING: OTHER WORKS BY CAROL SHIELDS

1. Shields is known for experimenting with point of view. Read her novels *Small Ceremonies* and *The Box Garden*, where she experiments with the points of view of both husband and wife — neither sees events in the same way. Do you see the complex multi-narrated technique of *The Stone Diaries* prefigured in these earlier novels?

2. The short story collection, *Various Miracles*, features memorable moments when the narrator illuminates the extraordinary interior of a character we would have otherwise thought completely ordinary. "Mrs. Turner Cutting the Grass" is an excellent example. Again, does such a technique — and a way of looking at humanity — seem an earlier version of the portrait of Daisy Flett in *The Stone Diaries*?

3. In her novel, *Larry's Party*, Shields writes from the male perspective. Do you find this technique sympathetic? convincing?

4. Shields seems to write against the current of postmodernism in her celebration of love between two unlikely people in *The Republic of Love*. Does such a feeling exist between Cuyler and Mercy Goodwill?

5. Shields's highly acclaimed (and her admitted favorite) novel, *Swann*, contains memorable experiments with both genre and point of view. Compare the techniques of this earlier novel with those in *The Stone Diaries*.

6. Read some of the essays from Shields's and Anderson's recent essay collection, *Dropped Threads* — including the essay by Shields's daughter, Anne Giardino. Shields has said, "Regarding the men overshadowing Daisy, I do think women were overshadowed then, of course, and I think they are overshadowed today. I don't think women have much of a chance, and my daughter has just written an article on this subject in *Dropped Threads*. And I do think she's right." Do you see evidence of this view in *The Stone Diaries*?

Notes

1. The Novelist

1. Eleanor Wachtel, 411

2. qtd. in Gussow, 2.

3. Werlock, "Interview With Carol Shields," March 25–28, 2001. Throughout this book, unless otherwise noted, all unascribed quotations from Carol Shields derive from this interview.

4. Sandra Coulson, "Shields Champions Tales of Ordinary People's Lives," *London Free Press*, Saturday, October 24, 1998, http://www.canoe.ca/JamBooksFeatures/shields_pulitzer.html;

5. Source: Database: *Contemporary Literary Criticism*. Gale Group, 2001.

6. Hollenberg, 4

7. Sturino, 1.

8. Solomon, 2.

9. Shields, "Framing the Structure," p. 3

10. CBC interview, 2001.

2. The Novel

11. Carol Shields, *The Stone Diaries*. New York: Penguin Putnam, 199—, pp. 5–6. All further references are to this edition and are parenthetically cited in the text.

12. "Daisy still manages to emerge as a kind of Everywoman" (Review of *The Stone Diaries*, *Books in Canada*, October 1993, vol. 22, no. 7, October, 1993, pp. 32–33. Internet full-text version, pp. 1–2. Journal Code: 0526. Parini [Internet 2].

13. Fitzgerald, 168 in *Contemporary Literary Criticism.*

14. Slethaus, Internet, p. 13.

15. Sims-Brandon, 1.

16. Mellor, 108.

17. Clara Thomas, 158.

18. Benedict, 3?. Internet page 2 of 3.

19. Marjory Fee, 179.

20. Mel Gussow, "A Celebrator of The Little Things," *New York Times*, Vol. CXLIV, No. 50057, May 10, 1995, p. B2. [email #16b and #90]. Internet full-text reproduction, pp. 1–3, c. 2001, The Gale Group. Source Database: *Contemporary Literary Criticism.*

3. The Novel's Reception

21. Sources for Section 3: qtd. in Diane Turbide, "A Prairie Pulitzer," *Maclean's*, v. 108 (May 1, 1995), pp. 76–77); *New York Times Book Review*, March 27, 1994; Clara Thomas, 159; Turbide, rev. of *The Stone Diaries*, 74; rev. of *The Stone Diaries*, *Books in Canada*, October 1993, vol. 22, no. 7, October, 1993, pp. 32–33; *Publisher's Weekly* December 13, 1993, v. 240, no. 50 p. 60 (2); *Times Literary Supplement* blurb on the list held by Bella Pomer, Carol Shields's agent; *Kirkus*, December 12, 1993; rev. of *The Stone Diaries*, *Books in Canada*, October 1993, vol. 22, no. 7, October, 1993, pp. 32–33. Internet full-text version, pp. 1–2. Journal Code: 0526.; Summers, 172; *People Weekly*, June 26, 1995 v. 43 No. 25, p. 32); *Mirabella*, March, 1994; Kirkus, December 12, 1993; *Reading*, March, 1994; Pomer's *Gentleman's Quarterly* blurb; *Mirabella*, March, 1994; *Publisher's Weekly*, December 13, 1993; *Reading*, March, 1994; see also *New York Times Book*

Review, March 27, 1994; *Publisher's Weekly,* December 13, 1993; *Times Literary Supplement*; Hughes, 40; Pomer's *Cosmopolitan* blurb; *New York Times Book Review,* March 27, 1994; Brookner, *The Spectator* 289; Brookner 167; Simone Vauthier, "Ruptures in Carol Shields's The Stone Diaries. *Anglophonia/Caliban,* 177–92; Winifred M. Mellor, "'The simple container of our existence': Narrative Ambiguity in Carol Shield's *The Stone Diaries.*" *Studies in Canadian Literature,* v. 20 (2), 1995, 97–110; Slethaug, Gordon E. "'The coded dots of life': Carol Shield's [sic] Diaries and Stones." *Canadian Literature,* Spring, 1988, vol. 156, 59–81. Internet full-text version pp. 1–17.

4. The Novel's Performance

22. Source for sales figure: Bella Pomer; source for international sales: Bella Pomer; Coulson, http://www.canoe.ca/JamBooksFeatures/shields_pulitzer.html; "Randall King, "Shields books bound for the silver screen," *Winnipeg Sun,* Wednesday, April 11, 2001: www.skicanadamag.com/JamBooks/apr11_carol-sun.html; Gordon Morash, *The Edmonton Journal,* www.edmontonjournal.com/entertainment/stories/991024/3041782.html+adaptations+of+books+by+carol+shields&hl=en; University of Vermont class website: http:www.uvm.edu/~english/fall2001.html; University of Pennsylvania class website: http:www.sas.upenn.edu/CGS/course_guide/2001A/engl.shtml; Wilder Penfield III, "Author Shields Wins Pulitzer," *Toronto Sun,* website: http://www.canoe.ca/JamBooksFeatures/shields_pulitzer.html

Bibliography

Works by Carol Shields

Others (poetry, 1972)
Intersect (poetry, 1974)
Susanna Moodie: Voice and Vision (critical study, 1976)
Small Ceremonies (novel, 1976)
The Box Garden (novel, 1977)
Happenstance (novel, 1980)
A Fairly Conventional Woman (novel, 1982)
Various Miracles (short stories, (1985)
Swann (novel, 1987)
The Orange Fish (short stories, 1990)
Departures and Arrivals (play, 1990)
A Celibate Season (novel, 1991), with Blanche Howard
The Republic of Love (novel, 1992)
Coming to Canada (poetry, 1992)
Thirteen Hands (drama, 1993)
Fashion, Power, Guilt and the Charity of Families (1993), with Caterine Shields
Scribner's Best of the Fiction Workshop (1998), edited by Carol Shields
The Stone Diaries (novel, 1993)
Larry's Party (novel, 1997)
Anniversary: A Comedy (1998), with Dave Williamson
Dressing Up for the Carnival (short stories, 2000)
Jane Austen (biography, 2001)
Dropped Threads (essay collection, 2001) co-edited with Marjorie Anderson
Penelope's Way (forthcoming, 2001), with Blanche Howard

Works about Carol Shields

Benedict, Elizabeth. "Below the Surface," Los Angeles Times Book Review, April 17, 1994, pp. 3, 7. Internet full-text version, c. 2001 by Gale Group. Source Database: Literature Resource Center, pp. 1–3 [email #12b and #100].

Brookner, Anita. "A Family and Its Good Fortune," *The Spectator*, Vol. 271, No. 8617, September 4, 1993, p. 289.

"Carol Shields: Conduct of Life." *Entertainment Weekly*, Dec. 22, 1995, no. 306, p. 61(1). Internet text version, p. 1. c. 2001 by Gale Group. Electronic Collection: Article A17884964.

Clayton, Laura Van Tuyl. "A Review of *The Stone Diaries*," *The Christian Science Monitor*, March 30, 1994, p. 19. Reprinted in *Contemporary Literary Criticism: Yearbook 1995*, vol. 91, pp. 174–75. Brigham Narins and Deborah A. Stanley, eds. Detroit, MI: Gale, 1995.

De Roo, Harvey. "A Little Like Flying: An Interview with Carol Shields." *West Coast Review*, Vol. 23, No. 3, Winter, 1988, pp. 38–56. Source: Internet full-text version, pp. 1–12, Contemporary Literary Criticism. c. 2001 by Gale Group.

Fee, Marjory. "Auto/Biographical Fictions," *Canadian Literature*, No. 144, Spring, 1995, pp. 173–74. Reprinted in *Contemporary Literary Criticism: Yearbook 1995*, vol. 91, pp. 179–80. Brigham Narins and Deborah A. Stanley, eds. Detroit, MI: Gale, 1995.

Fitzgerald, Penelope. "Sunny Side Up," London Review of Books, vol. 15, No. 17, September 9, 1993, p. 19. Reprinted in *Contemporary Literary Criticism: Yearbook 1995*, vol. 91, pp. 168–69. Brigham Narins and Deborah A. Stanley, Eds. Detroit, MI: Gale, 1995.[email #11c and #92]

Gillespie, Elgy. "Carol Shields: Life in America (Canada and France has influenced her Booker-nominated Fiction). PW Interviews. *Publisher's Weekly*, Feb. 28, 1994, v. 241, no. 9, p. 61(2), p. 62). (duplicate—electronic version?

Gussow, Mel. "A Celebrator of The Little Things," New York Times, Vol. CXLIV, No. 50057, May 10, 1995, p. B2. [email #16b and #90]. Internet full-text reproduction, pp. 1–3, c. 2001, The Gale Group. Source Database: Contemporary Literary Criticism.

Hollenberg, Donna. "An Interview With Carol Shields." *Contemporary Literature*, Fall 1998, v. 39 no. 3, pp. 338–56. Internet full-text version, pp. 1–11. c. 2001 by Gale Group. Electronic Collection: Article A21229909.

Hughes, Kathryn. "*The Stone Diaries*," New Statesman and Society, August 20, 1993, p. 40(1). [email #14]

Kaufman, Joanne. "Late Bloomer," *People Weekly*, June 26, 1995, v . 43 n. 25, p. 32. [email #66]

King, Nicola. "Carol Shields: Overview." In *Contemporary Popular Writers*, Dave Mote, ed. St. James Press, 1997. c. 2001 by Gale Group. Internet text version, pp. 1–2.

Koenig, Rhoda, "Rock-Solid, Stone-Cold," *New York Magazine*, Vol. 27, No. 10, March 7, 1994, p. 62. Reprinted in *Contemporary Literary Criticism: Yearbook 1995*, vol. 91, pp. 172–73. Brigham Narins and Deborah A. Stanley, eds. Detroit, MI: Gale, 1995.

Life and Times: Carol Shields. CBC Documentary. Directed by Anna Benson Giles and Charles Mapleson. C. Malachite, Ltd., c. 2001.

McGill, Allyson F. "A Tangle of Underground Streams," *Belles Lettres: A Review of Books by Women*, Vol. 10, No. 1, Fall, 1994, pp. 32, 34. Reprinted in *Contemporary Literary Criticism: Yearbook 1995*, vol. 91, pp. 175–76. Brigham Narins and Deborah A. Stanley, eds. Detroit, MI: Gale, 1995.

Mellor, Winifred M. "'The simple container of our existence': Narrative Ambiguity in Carol Shield's *The Stone Diaries*." *Studies in Canadian Literature*, v. 20 (2), 1995, 97–110.

Messud, Claire. "Redeemed by an Act of Imagination," *Manchester Guardian Weekly*, October 3, 1993, p. 28. Reprinted in *Contemporary Literary Criticism: Yearbook 1995*, vol. 91, pp. 1170–71. Brigham Narins and Deborah A. Stanley, eds. Detroit, MI: Gale, 1995.

"Neighbors to the North." *Publishers Weekly*, September 25, 1995, v. 242, n. 39 p. 16 (1). Internet text version, p. 1. c. 2001 by Gale Group. Article A17474379.

Parini, Jay. "Men and Women, Forever Misaligned," New York Times Book Review, March 27, 1994, pp. 3, 14. Reprinted in *Contemporary Literary Criticism: Yearbook 1995*, vol. 91, pp. 173–74. Brigham Narins and Deborah A. Stanley, eds. Detroit, MI: Gale, 1995.

People Weekly, June 26, 1995 v. 43 No. 25, p. 32. [email: #67]

Pool, Gail. "Review of Carol Shields's *Happenstance* and *The Stone Diaries*," *Women's Review of Books*, Vol. XI, No. 8, May, 1994, p. 20. [email #25 and 91]. Internet full-text version, pp. 1–4, c. 2001 by the Gale Group. source: Contemporary Literary Criticism.

"Revealed: Personal Milestones," *Maclean's*, May 3, 1999. Internet full-text version, 1–2. Electronic Collection: A54486208.

Review of *The Stone Diaries*, *Books in Canada*, October 1993, vol. 22, no. 7, October, 1993, pp. 32–33. Internet full-text version, pp. 1–2. Journal Code: 0526.

Shaman, Geraldine. "Straining to Fulfill Ambitions," The Globe and Mail, Toronto, October 2, 1993, p. C23. Reprinted in *Contemporary Literary Criticism: Yearbook 1995*, vol. 91, pp. 169–70. Brigham Narins and Deborah A. Stanley, eds. Detroit, MI: Gale, 1995.

Shields, Carol. "Framing the Structure of a Novel." *The Writer*, July 1998, v. 111 no. 7, pp. 3(4). Internet full-text version, pp. 1–4. c. 2001 by Gale Group. Electronic Collection: Article A20790979.

Sims-Brandon, Lisa. "Revisiting Sleepy Hollow: An Analysis of Edna in *The Awakening* and Daisy in *The Stone Diaries*," journal article, 1–5. [email #106]

Slethaug, Gordon E. "'The coded dots of life': Carol Shield's [sic] Diaries and Stones." *Canadian Literature*, Spring, 1988, vol. 156, 59–81. Internet full-text version pp. 1–17.

Solomon, Andy. "Carol Shields: Overview." In *Contemporary Novelists*, 6th ed. Susan Windisch Brown, ed. St. James Press, 1996. c. 2001 by Gale Group. Internet text version, pp. 1–3.

Sturino, Ida. "An Interview With Carol Shields," *Scrivener*, Spring, 1995, pp. 76–85. Internet full-text version, Source: Contemporary Literary Criticism, c. 2001 by the Gale Group, pp. 1–6.

Summers, Merna. "Small is Beautiful," *Canadian Forum*, vol. 72, no. 826, Jan.–Feb., 1994, pp. 44–45. Reprinted in *Contemporary Literary Criticism: Yearbook 1995*, vol. 91, pp. 171–72. Brigham Narins and Deborah A. Stanley, eds. Detroit, MI: Gale, 1995.

Thomas, Clara. "Carol Shields: *The Republic of Love* and *The Stone Diaries*. 'Swerves of Destiny' and 'Rings of Light'." In *Union in Partition: Essays in Honour of Jeanne Delbaere*. Gilbert Debusscher and Marc Maufort, eds. — — —: 1997, pp. 153–60.

Thomas, Joan. "The Golden Book: An Interview with Carol Shields," Prairie Fire, Winter 93–94, 54–62.

Turbide, Diane. "A Prairie Pulitzer," *Maclean's*, v. 108 (May 1, 1995), pp. 76–77. Internet text version, pp. 1–3. c. 2001 by Gale Group. First Search c. 1992–2001. OCLC Electronic Collection.

———. "*The Stone Diaries*," Maclean's, October 11, 1993, vol. 106, no. 41, p. 74(1). [email #13 and #74]

Vauthier, Simone. "Ruptures in Carol Shields's *The Stone Diaries*. *Anglophonia/ Caliban*, 177–92.

Wachtel, Eleanor. "Interview With Carol Shields," Room of One's Own 13, No. 1–2 (1989), 5–45. Reprinted in *Contemporary Literary Criticism: Yearbook 1995*, vol. 113, pp. 409–15. Jeffrey W. Hunter, Deborah A. Schmitt, and Timothy J. White,, Eds. Detroit, MI: Gale, 1998.

Werlock, Abby H. P. "Interview With Carol Shields." This interview took place during two telephone calls on 25 and 28 March, 2001.